NEWTON
VS
LEIBNIZ

Newton vs Leibniz

Calculus Controversy

RAFEAL MECHLORE

UNIEK ENTERPRISES

Contents

INDEX

Introduction:

1. Setting the stage for the intense historical dispute between Isaac Newton and Gottfried Wilhelm Leibniz.
2. The broader context of the scientific revolution in the 17th century.
3. Previewing the profound impact of the calculus controversy on mathematics and science.

Chapter 1: The Birth of Calculus
1.1 An introduction to the early development of calculus and its necessity in solving real-world problems.
1.2 Historical figures who contributed to the groundwork for calculus, including Archimedes, Fermat, and Descartes.
1.3 The need for a systematic mathematical framework to describe change and motion.

Chapter 2: Newton's Method of Fluxions
2.1 Isaac Newton's early life, education, and scientific endeavors.
2.2 In-depth exploration of Newton's method of "the calculus of fluents" or "fluxions."
2.3 Newton's mathematical innovations, including the Fundamental Theorem of Calculus.

Chapter 3: Leibniz's Infinitesimal Calculus
3.1 Gottfried Wilhelm Leibniz's background, influences, and intellectual pursuits.
3.2 Leibniz's development of the "calculus" using notation based on differentials and infinitesimals.

3.3A comparison of Leibniz's and Newton's notations and approaches to calculus.

Chapter 4: The Priority Dispute Begins

4.1The emergence of accusations of plagiarism and priority between Newton and Leibniz.

4.2Correspondence and publications that fueled the controversy.

4.3The role of the Royal Society and other mathematicians in the dispute.

Chapter 5: The Royal Society's Verdict

5.1Examination of the Royal Society's investigation into the priority dispute.

5.2The findings and conclusions of the Royal Society's report.

5.3The impact of the Royal Society's decision on the reputations of Newton and Leibniz.

Chapter 6: International Controversy and Legacy

6.1The spread of the calculus controversy beyond England and Germany.

6.2The reactions of mathematicians and scholars across Europe.

6.3The lasting legacy of the dispute on mathematics, notation, and calculus education.

Chapter 7: Beyond Calculus: The Mathematicians' Other Contributions

7.1A look at the broader contributions of Newton and Leibniz to mathematics and science.

7.2Newton's laws of motion, universal gravitation, and his impact on physics.

7.3Leibniz's work in philosophy, logic, and contributions to various fields.

Chapter 8: Cultural and Philosophical Implications

8.1The calculus controversy's cultural and philosophical implications.

8.2The contrast between Newton's empiricism and Leibniz's rationalism.

8.3How the dispute reflected broader intellectual trends of the time.

Chapter 9: The Legacy of the Calculus Controversy

9.1Summarizing the enduring significance of the Newton vs. Leibniz calculus controversy.

9.2Reflecting on how their rivalry advanced mathematics and science.

9.3The continued relevance of their contributions in contemporary mathematics.

INTRODUCTION

In the records of logical history, not many questions have lighted as much enthusiasm, interest, and scholarly enthusiasm as the unpleasant quarrel between Sir Isaac Newton and Gottfried Wilhelm Leibniz over the creation of analytics. This debate, which unfurled during the late seventeenth hundred years, is a demonstration of the intricacies and nuances of human imagination and logical disclosure. While math is presently viewed as one of the most principal parts of science, its introduction to the world was damaged by extraordinary contentions, allegations of counterfeiting, and a significant conflict of inner selves.

Newton and Leibniz, two splendid personalities of their time, freely fostered their own strategies for analytics. Their equal commitments, however unmistakable in approach, established the groundwork for current arithmetic and science. This discussion, frequently alluded to as the "Math Need Debate," is an enamoring story of virtuoso, desire, and the journey for scholarly incomparability.

This account will dive profound into the lives, foundations, and scholarly excursions of these two titans of arithmetic and science. It will investigate the verifiable setting that formed their work, the improvement of math as a numerical discipline, and the different elements that added to the rancorous question among Newton and Leibniz. To really comprehend this debate, we should set out on an excursion through the logical, philosophical, and individual scenes of the late seventeenth 100 years.

At the core of this discussion lies the significant inquiry: Who really merits recognition for the innovation of analytics, Newton or Leibniz? Each side had its lifelong fans and heartfelt naysayers. In the hundreds of years that followed, antiquarians, mathematicians, and researchers enthusiastically took apart the proof and discussed the benefits of each case. While the debate is for some time got comfortable the eyes of the numerical local area, the tradition of Newton and Leibniz keeps on charming the individuals who look to figure out the complexities of logical revelation.

This story means to give a far reaching investigation of the Newton versus Leibniz analytics debate, revealing insight into the lives and commitments of these two unprecedented people while unwinding the unpredictable strings of this notable question. Through this excursion, we will come to see the value in the splendor of these

mathematicians as well as the persevering through effect of their work on the universe of science and arithmetic.

1. Setting the stage for the intense historical dispute between Isaac Newton and Gottfried Wilhelm Leibniz.

   The stage for the serious verifiable debate between Isaac Newton and Gottfried Wilhelm Leibniz over the development of analytics was set against the background of the late seventeenth 100 years, a period portrayed by a thriving interest in math, science, and reasoning. This period, set apart by scholarly age, established the groundwork for the improvement of analytics and, accidentally, for the unpleasant contention that would follow.

   The Renaissance and the Logical Insurgency:

   The late seventeenth century was a result of the Renaissance and the Logical Insurgency, two epochal developments that reshaped the scholarly scene of Europe. The Renaissance had revived interest in traditional information, supporting a feeling of request and an interest with the numerical thoughts of old Greece. This restoration of numerical idea was instrumental in rousing people in the future of mathematicians, including Newton and Leibniz.

   The Forerunners of Analytics:

   Before the conventional advancement of analytics, numerical trailblazers like Johannes Kepler, Pierre de Fermat, and René Descartes had laid the basis for the discipline. Kepler's laws of planetary movement and Fermat's strategy for finding digression lines were early antecedents to the thoughts of analytics. In the mean time, Descartes' direction calculation gave an imperative scaffold among variable based math and math, offering new devices for numerical investigation.

   Newton's Initial Life and Instruction:

   Isaac Newton, brought into the world on January 4, 1643, in Woolsthorpe, Britain, showed early indications of numerical virtuoso. In any case, his life was not without difficulty. Stranded early in life, Newton's early stages were set apart by neediness and a profound feeling of seclusion. By the by, he selected at Trinity School,

Cambridge, in 1661, where he experienced crafted by the main mathematicians of the time, including Descartes and Fermat.

Newton's advantage in arithmetic was lighted during his time at Cambridge, where he consumed the standards of variable based math and calculation and started to investigate the early field of analytics. His initial journals uncover his interest with the technique for indivisibles, an antecedent to indispensable math, as well as his work on the binomial hypothesis.

Leibniz's Initial Life and Training:

On the European mainland, a youthful polymath named Gottfried Wilhelm Leibniz was likewise arising as a numerical wonder. Brought into the world on July 1, 1646, in Leipzig, Germany, Leibniz showed extraordinary scholarly interest since the beginning. His schooling in regulation and reasoning drove him to the investigation of math, and he immediately leaving his imprint with a progression of imaginative thoughts.

Leibniz's mission for a general language to address information drove him to foster a twofold numeral framework and a mechanical number cruncher, exhibiting his tendency toward numerical reflection. He sought after different roads of exploration, including the investigation of boundless series and the thought of "differential triangles," which foreshadowed key ideas in differential math.

The Mission for a Widespread Science:

Both Newton and Leibniz were attracted to making a widespread numerical language that could portray normal peculiarities with accuracy. This common desire was a demonstration of the scholarly environment of their time, where researchers across Europe tried to bind together information and make frameworks of felt that rose above disciplinary limits.

The longing to open the insider facts of the regular world was a strong inspiration. Newton, for example, was enraptured by the issue of divine mechanics and looked for numerical devices to portray the movement of planets and heavenly bodies. Leibniz, then again, imagined a more broad structure for understanding change and variety, which he accepted could be applied to fields as different as material science, financial matters, and theory.

Autonomous Disclosures and Advancement:

The way to math was cleared with free revelations by both Newton and Leibniz. Newton's strategy for "the fluxions" and "the technique for extreme proportions" was imagined during the 1660s, while Leibniz fostered his variant of analytics, known as "minuscule math," in the last part of the 1670s and mid 1680s. The two mathematicians, uninformed about one another's work, were making momentous commitments to the field.

Newton's way to deal with math included the idea of prompt paces of progress, which he called "fluxions." He utilized the strategy for cutoff points to ascertain these amounts, making way for present day differential analytics. Leibniz, then again, presented the documentation of the necessary sign (∫) and utilized the possibility of infinitesimals, little

amounts that could be utilized to ascertain slants and regions, hence establishing the groundwork for basic analytics.

The Test of Attribution:

As Newton and Leibniz kept on fostering their individual analytics strategies, they started to distribute their discoveries. The test of attribution, be that as it may, posed a potential threat. The scholarly local area of the time was separated in its acknowledgment of their commitments. Newton's works, introduced in the "Strategy for Fluxions" and the "Principia Mathematica," were written in Latin, restricting their openness. Leibniz, then again, distributed his thoughts in a more discernible structure in French and Latin, procuring him more extensive acknowledgment.

The contention among English and Mainland mathematicians further muddled matters. The English mathematicians, who leaned toward Newton's work, were leaned to excuse Leibniz as a liar, while the Continentals, drove by the Bernoulli family, embraced Leibniz's documentation and techniques.

The Job of Need:

The idea of need, the possibility that the principal individual to find or distribute a specific thought ought to be credited, turned into a main issue of dispute. Newton accepted that he had found math first and blamed Leibniz for having replicated his thoughts. Leibniz, then again, contended that he had created analytics autonomously and that Newton had not distributed his work until some other time.

The Illustrious Society's Examination:

The question raised when Newton, who had turned into the Leader of the Imperial Society in 1703, utilized his situation to send off an examination concerning Leibniz's cases of need. This examination, known as the "Analytics Need Question," further stressed the connection between the two mathematicians and their individual allies.

Heritage and Effect:

The tradition of this extraordinary verifiable question is significant. While it eventually discolored the notorieties of both Newton and Leibniz, it additionally featured the meaning of their commitments to math. The documentation presented by Leibniz, especially the necessary sign (∫) and the utilization of dx and dy, became standard in numerical documentation and is as yet utilized today. Newton's idea of fluxions and his strategies for limits keep on being central in the investigation of math.

Eventually, the math discussion helps us that the pursuit to remember information is many times a chaotic and combative undertaking. It highlights the human components of aspiration, self image, and contest that can shape the course of logical disclosure.

Regardless of the unpleasant debates and individual hostilities, both Newton and Leibniz made exceptional commitments to the advancement of analytics, enhancing the universe of math and science all the while.

In the ensuing segments of this story, we will dig further into the lives and works of Isaac Newton and Gottfried Wilhelm Leibniz, following the development of their thoughts and the unpredictable snare of conditions that prompted the extreme verifiable argument about the creation of math.

2. **The broader context of the scientific revolution in the 17th century.**

The seventeenth century was a period of significant change in the realm of science and reasoning, set apart by a period known as the Logical Upset. This time, spreading over generally from the late sixteenth 100 years to the mid eighteenth hundred years, saw an extreme change in the manner in which people apparent and grasped the normal world. The Logical Upset laid the foundation for present day science and was described by a progression of scholarly turns of events, disclosures, and outlook changes that eternity modified the direction of mankind's set of experiences.

The Renaissance Roots:

The starting points of the Logical Upheaval can be followed back to the Renaissance, a social and scholarly development that started in Italy in the fourteenth 100 years and progressively spread all through Europe. During the Renaissance, there was a restoration of interest in the old style information on the Greeks and Romans, prompting a recharged appreciation for science, stargazing, and regular way of thinking.

Figures like Leonardo da Vinci, who succeeded in both artistic expression and technical disciplines, exemplified the Renaissance soul of interest and interdisciplinary investigation. This period established the groundwork for a more exact and observational way to deal with grasping the world, as well as a developing accentuation on human explanation.

The Copernican Insurgency:

One of the original occasions that set up for the Logical Transformation was the Copernican Unrest, started by Nicolaus Copernicus in the mid sixteenth hundred years. Copernicus tested the geocentric model of the universe that had won for north of a thousand years, proposing rather a heliocentric model in which the Earth spun around the Sun. This momentous hypothesis upset stargazing as well as represented a crucial test to laid out power, as it went against strict and philosophical convictions of the time.

The distribution of Copernicus' "De revolutionibus orbium coelestium" in 1543 denoted a critical defining moment, laying the preparation for a more proof based way to deal with grasping the universe.

Galileo Galilei and the Telescope:

Crafted by Galileo Galilei in the mid seventeenth century further impelled the Logical Transformation. Galileo's utilization of the telescope to mention cosmic observable facts, like the periods of Venus and the moons of Jupiter, gave undeniable proof on the side of the Copernican heliocentric model. His exact way to deal with science, which underlined perception and trial and error, established the groundwork for present day physical science.

Notwithstanding, Galileo's support for the heliocentric model and his conflict with the Catholic Church over issues of power and understanding of sacred writing likewise featured the pressures among science and laid out strict precepts. Regardless of confronting mistreatment, Galileo's work significantly affected the progression of logical idea.

The Numerical Transformation:

Simultaneously with improvements in space science, the seventeenth century saw a numerical transformation that enormously impacted the Logical Unrest. Mathematicians like René Descartes, Pierre de Fermat, and John Napier made huge commitments to the field. Descartes' improvement of direction calculation, wherein mathematical shapes could be addressed logarithmically, was a critical stage towards the unification of math and the actual sciences.

Moreover, the creation of logarithms by John Napier and Fermat's work on the analytics of maxima and minima made ready for the later advancement of math by figures like Isaac Newton and Gottfried Wilhelm Leibniz.

The Logical Strategy and Induction:

Vital to the Logical Insurgency was the rise of the logical strategy, an orderly way to deal with request and trial and error. Francis Bacon, frequently viewed as the dad of induction, pushed for the assortment of exact information through cautious perception and trial and error. His work established the philosophical starting point for the observational and trial strategies that became essential to present day science.

Bacon's contemporary, René Descartes, accentuated the significance of uncertainty and doubt chasing information. His renowned assertion, "Cogito, thus total" (I think, in this way I'm), highlighted the meaning of individual explanation and uncertainty as a reason for logical request.

Isaac Newton and the Laws of Movement:

Maybe one of the most notorious figures of the Logical Upheaval was Sir Isaac Newton. Newton's momentous work, "Numerical Standards of Normal Way of thinking" (1687), introduced his laws of movement and the law of general attraction. These regulations gave a far reaching and numerically thorough structure for grasping the movement of items on The planet and in the sky.

Newton's work joined earthly and heavenly mechanics as well as shown the force of science in depicting normal peculiarities. His idea of widespread attractive energy, which expressed that each item in the universe draws in each and every article with a power relative to their masses and conversely corresponding to the square of the distance between them, was a great accomplishment.

The Illumination and the Spread of Thoughts:

The Logical Upset likewise met with the more extensive Edification, a scholarly development of the eighteenth century that underlined reason, independence, and the potential for progress through schooling and the spread of information. Edification masterminds like Voltaire, Denis Diderot, and Jean-Jacques Rousseau supported the standards of science, secularism, and the division of chapel and state.

The distribution of the "Encyclopédie" altered by Diderot and D'Alembert, a summary of information crossing different disciplines, mirrored the Edification's obligation to dispersing data and advancing decisive reasoning.

The Tradition of the Logical Upheaval:

The Logical Upheaval made a permanent imprint on mankind's set of experiences. It changed the manner in which we see and connect with the normal world, cultivating a feeling of request and observational examination that keeps on forming logical trains today. The advancement of the logical technique, the numerical unrest, and the heliocentric model of the universe established the groundwork for the cutting edge logical undertaking.

Additionally, the Logical Insurgency had broad cultural and philosophical ramifications. It tested customary strict and philosophical specialists, introducing a period where experimental proof and reason outweighed authoritative opinion and strange notion. This change in thinking added to the headway of information as well as laid the preparation for the Illumination and the resulting Time of Reason.

3. Previewing the profound impact of the calculus controversy on mathematics and science.

The math debate, frequently outlined as the harsh question between Isaac Newton and Gottfried Wilhelm Leibniz over the development of analytics, was something beyond a verifiable disagreement between two splendid personalities. It enduringly affected the fields of math and science, molding the direction of these disciplines in manners that keep on reverberating today. In this investigation, we'll see the sweeping outcomes of this debate, from the advancement of thorough numerical establishments to its suggestions for logical procedure and coordinated effort.

Advancement of Thorough Numerical Establishments:

At the core of the math discussion was a discussion over documentation and strategy. Newton and Leibniz moved toward math from various points, prompting the advancement of unmistakable notational frameworks. While Newton utilized "fluxions" and the "technique for extreme proportions," Leibniz presented the vital sign ($\int$) and the documentation dx and dy. This variety of documentations at first made disarray at the end of the day prodded a more profound comprehension of the ideas in question.

The need to accommodate and formalize these documentations prompted the making of thorough numerical starting points for analytics. Mathematicians of the time, like Augustin-Louis Cauchy and Karl Weierstrass, chipped away at refining and explaining the standards of analytics, prompting the foundation of epsilon-delta definitions and the idea of cut-off points. These central improvements settled the notational questions as well as laid the basis for a more thorough and methodical way to deal with math.

Progressions in Numerical Meticulousness and Confirmation Hypothesis:

The math discussion assumed a critical part in the development of numerical thoroughness and verification hypothesis. As the debate among

Newton and Leibniz seethed on, mathematicians perceived the requirement for exact definitions and proverbial frameworks to support their work. This prompted the improvement of formal numerical verifications and the rise of numerical thoroughness as a foundation of the discipline.

Trailblazers like Leonhard Euler and Richard Dedekind added to this shift towards thorough confirmation hypothesis. Euler's work on boundless series and Dedekind's commitments to number hypothesis and set hypothesis mirrored a pledge to intelligent consistency and numerical meticulousness that keeps on impacting contemporary science.

Normalization of Numerical Documentation:

The math contention provoked a push for normalization in numerical documentation. To keep away from the disarray emerging from the different notational frameworks of Newton and Leibniz, mathematicians looked for shared conviction. This attempt prompted the foundation of generally acknowledged images and shows for addressing numerical ideas.

Leibniz's fundamental documentation, for example, turned out to be generally taken on and stays the norm for addressing combination in arithmetic today. The unification of numerical documentation added to more noteworthy lucidity and cognizance in numerical talk, making it simpler for mathematicians across societies and dialects to successfully convey their thoughts.

Advancement of Coordinated effort and Companion Survey:

The math discussion additionally highlighted the significance of joint effort and friend audit in the logical cycle. The debate among Newton and Leibniz was not just a question of individual contention but rather an impression of the more extensive logical and scholarly environment of the time, where contending claims frequently continued without some kind of restraint.

Accordingly, foundations, for example, the Illustrious Society in Britain and the Berlin Foundation in Prussia started to stress the significance of companion audit and free confirmation of logical cases. This shift towards a more cooperative and basically evaluative way to deal with logical exploration laid out the standards of current logical practice, where speculations and disclosures are exposed to thorough examination prior to being acknowledged as a component of the logical ordinance.

Impact on Different Areas of Science:

The analytics discussion had expansive ramifications past science. It impacted the improvement of material science, designing, and other logical disciplines. Newton's work on math, for instance, assumed an essential part in his definition of the laws of movement and the law of widespread attraction, which established the groundwork for old style physical science.

Furthermore, the techniques and ideas of analytics tracked down applications in assorted logical fields, from stargazing and mechanics to science and financial aspects. This cross-fertilization of thoughts and strategies sped up the progression of science by giving amazing assets to displaying and grasping regular peculiarities.

Empowering Scholarly Power and Discussion:

While the math debate was set apart by bitterness and questions, it likewise filled in as a demonstration of the scholarly energy of the time. The discussion over need and documentation prodded extreme insightful commitment and urged mathematicians and researchers to survey and refine their thoughts basically.

Scholarly discussions, in any event, when combative, can be impetuses for progress. The math discussion tested laid out doctrines and pushed the limits of human information, cultivating a climate of scholarly interest and request that keeps on being a main impetus in logical disclosure.

Rousing People in the future:

The math contention made a permanent imprint on the historical backdrop of science and math, and its stories have motivated innumerable ages of understudies, mathematicians, and researchers. It fills in as an update that even the most splendid personalities can wrestle with vulnerabilities and conflicts in their quest for information.

Besides, the debate highlights the significance of modesty notwithstanding scholarly difficulties. Both Newton and Leibniz made stupendous commitments to human comprehension, but they were not reliable. Their debate fills in as an update that no thought ought to be taken as doctrine, and the logical strategy requires a continuous obligation to wariness and basic assessment.

Chapter 1

Chapter 1

The Birth of Calculus

The introduction of math denotes an essential crossroads throughout the entire existence of math and science. This notable discipline, which upset the manner in which we comprehend and portray our general surroundings, was freely evolved by two splendid personalities, Sir Isaac Newton and Gottfried Wilhelm Leibniz, during the late seventeenth 100 years. Their disclosures, while unmistakable in approach, established the groundwork for present day math and science. In this thorough investigation of the introduction of analytics, we will dive profound into the lives, foundations, and scholarly excursions of these two titans of arithmetic. We will likewise look at the verifiable setting that molded their work, the improvement of math as a numerical discipline, and the persevering through tradition of their commitments.

Forerunners to Analytics

Prior to diving into crafted by Newton and Leibniz, understanding the numerical scene that went before the introduction of calculus is fundamental. A few forerunners and essential thoughts made ready for the improvement of this earth shattering discipline.

1.1 Antiquated Science:

The antiquated Greeks, especially mathematicians like Eudoxus and Archimedes, made critical commitments to the investigation of calculation and analytics like ideas. Archimedes, for example, determined regions and volumes utilizing a strategy likened to essential math, laying an early preparation for the discipline.

1.2 The Strategy for Depletion:

Old mathematicians utilized a strategy known as the "technique for depletion" to surmised regions and volumes. This technique included separating a shape into more modest parts and adding their regions, an idea firmly connected with reconciliation.

1.3 Archaic Islamic Mathematicians:

During the archaic period, Islamic mathematicians, for example, Ibn al-Haytham and Alhazen made progress in understanding optics and the properties of light, which had suggestions for the investigation of minute amounts.

1.4 The Renaissance and the Recovery of Arithmetic:

The Renaissance time frame, with its recovery of old style information, started reestablished interest in arithmetic. Figures like Leonardo da Vinci and Niccolò Tartaglia laid the basis for future improvements by investigating numerical ideas.

The Early Life and Training of Isaac Newton

To comprehend the introduction of math, we should initially investigate the life and scholarly advancement of Sir Isaac Newton, one of the prime supporters of analytics.

2.1 Early Life and Training:

Isaac Newton was brought into the world on January 4, 1643, in Woolsthorpe, Britain. His initial life was set apart by misfortune, as he was stranded early on. Regardless of these difficulties, he entered Trinity School, Cambridge, in 1661, where he experienced crafted by noticeable mathematicians like René Descartes and John Wallis.

2.2 Impacts and Motivations:

Newton's time at Cambridge presented him to an abundance of numerical thoughts. He drenched himself in the investigation of polynomial math, calculation, and early analytics antecedents, making way for his future leap forwards.

2.3 The Strategy for Fluxions:

During the 1660s, while still a youthful researcher, Newton started fostering his strategy for "the fluxions." This creative methodology planned to grasp change and movement through tiny amounts. The technique for fluxions laid the basis for present day differential analytics.

The Early Life and Schooling of Gottfried Wilhelm Leibniz

In lined up with Newton's excursion, Gottfried Wilhelm Leibniz left on his own scholarly investigation that would prompt the improvement of analytics.

3.1 Early Life and Training:

Leibniz was brought into the world on July 1, 1646, in Leipzig, Germany. Like Newton, he showed scholarly interest since the beginning. He sought after a different training in regulation and theory, which drove him to math.

3.2 Advancements and Numerical Pursuits:

Leibniz's journey for a widespread language to address information drove him to make a double numeral framework and a mechanical mini-computer. These early innovations exhibited his tendency toward numerical reflection.

3.3 Differential Analytics:

Leibniz's investigation of boundless series and the idea of "differential triangles" foreshadowed key components of differential analytics. He fostered another documentation for analytics, including the vital sign ($\int$) and the utilization of dx and dy, which stay standard in numerical documentation today.

Autonomous Disclosures and the Introduction of Math

As both Newton and Leibniz freely chipped away at their renditions of math, the stage was set for the introduction of this pivotal discipline.

4.1 Equal Turns of events:

Newton's strategy for "the fluxions" and Leibniz's "minuscule analytics" were considered freely in the late seventeenth 100 years. Their methodologies were unmistakable, however both intended to address the crucial ideas of movement, change, and rates.

4.2 Distribution and Acknowledgment:

Newton and Leibniz started distributing their discoveries, igniting acknowledgment and interest inside the numerical local area. The test of attribution and need before long arose, as every mathematician guaranteed credit for the innovation of analytics.

The Analytics Discussion

The introduction of math was damaged by serious contentions, allegations of copyright infringement, and a significant conflict of inner selves. The resulting math contention stays a spellbinding story of virtuoso, desire, and the journey for scholarly incomparability.

5.1 Allegations of Counterfeiting:

The analytics contention arrived at its pinnacle as Newton blamed Leibniz for having duplicated his thoughts. Leibniz, thus, fervently guarded his free commitments, attesting that he had created math without information on Newton's work.

5.2 The Job of Need:

The idea of need, the possibility that the principal individual to find or distribute a specific thought ought to be attributed, became key to the contention. It partitioned the numerical local area, with English mathematicians inclining toward Newton and Continentals embracing Leibniz's documentation and strategies.

5.3 The Imperial Society's Examination:

Newton, as Leader of the Imperial Society, utilized his situation to send off an examination concerning Leibniz's cases of need. This examination, known as the "Analytics Need Debate," extended the hostility between the two mathematicians and their individual allies.

Heritage and Effect of Math

The analytics contention might have blurred into history, however its inheritance perseveres, significantly forming the universes of math and science.

6.1 Normalization of Documentation:

The discussion provoked the normalization of numerical documentation, with Leibniz's indispensable sign ($\int$) and differential documentation (dx and dy) turning out to be generally embraced. These notational shows keep on being fundamental in math today.

6.2 Advancement of Numerical Thoroughness:

Mathematicians, for example, Augustin-Louis Cauchy and Karl Weierstrass refined and formalized the standards of analytics, presenting epsilon-delta definitions and the idea of cutoff points. This thorough establishment settled notational debates and prepared for current math.

6.3 Logical Procedure and Coordinated effort:

The contention featured the significance of coordinated effort and companion survey in logical request. Establishments like the Imperial Society and the Berlin Foundation underlined the requirement for free check and basic assessment of logical cases.

6.4 Effect on Different Fields:

Analytics, conceived out of the debate, had significant ramifications past arithmetic. It assumed a vital part in the improvement of material science, designing, and other logical disciplines. Newton's laws of movement and attraction, established in analytics, established the groundwork for traditional physical science.

6.5 Motivation for People in the future:

The math debate fills in as a demonstration of the intricacies and difficulties of logical disclosure. It motivates people in the future of mathematicians and researchers, accentuating the significance of modesty, distrust, and decisive reasoning chasing after information.

1.1 An introduction to the early development of calculus and its necessity in solving real-world problems.

Analytics, frequently portrayed as the science of progress and movement, is a central part of math that has significantly influenced the manner in which we comprehend and communicate with the world. Its turn of events, which occurred during the late seventeenth hundred years, was a reaction to the developing requirement for numerical instruments to address complex true issues. In this investigation of the early improvement of math, we will travel back so as to a period set apart by scholarly interest, logical upheaval, and the development of two splendid personalities, Isaac Newton and Gottfried Wilhelm Leibniz. We will analyze the verifiable setting that required the production of analytics and investigate its basic job in taking care of true issues.

The Scholarly Scene of the seventeenth Hundred years

To see the value in the early advancement of math, we should initially set the stage by grasping the scholarly environment of the seventeenth 100 years. This was a period portrayed by momentous headways in science, math, and reasoning.

1.1 The Renaissance and Rediscovery of Science:

The Renaissance, a social and scholarly development that started in Italy in the fourteenth hundred years, prompted a restored interest underway of old Greek mathematicians. Researchers rediscovered and interpreted antiquated texts, including crafted by Euclid and Archimedes, which laid the foundation for the advancement of math.

1.2 The Logical Unrest:

The seventeenth century saw the Logical Upset, a change in outlook in the manner in which people moved toward the normal world. Figures like Galileo Galilei and Johannes Kepler tested winning convictions and made ready for a more exact, exploratory, and numerical way to deal with grasping nature.

1.3 The Job of Calculation:

Calculation, long thought to be the zenith of numerical accomplishment, was fundamental to the logical undertakings of the time. Descartes' improvement of scientific calculation, which permitted mathematical conditions to portray mathematical shapes, set up for the mix of variable based math and calculation, a major part of analytics.

Isaac Newton - The Introduction of Differential Analytics

The early improvement of math found one of its trailblazers in Sir Isaac Newton, whose work established the groundwork for differential analytics.

2.1 Newton's Initial Life and Instruction:

Isaac Newton, brought into the world on January 4, 1643, in Woolsthorpe, Britain, showed early indications of numerical virtuoso. In spite of a difficult youth set apart by destitution and misfortune, he selected at Trinity School, Cambridge, where he experienced crafted by mathematicians like René Descartes and John Wallis.

2.2 The Strategy for Fluxions:

Newton's progressive way to deal with analytics, known as "the technique for fluxions," was created during the 1660s. This strategy meant to comprehend quick paces of progress, an idea that demonstrated fundamental in portraying movement and change in the actual world.

2.3 Application to True Issues:

Newton's work on differential math significantly affected technical studies. His strategy considered the exact portrayal of paces of progress in different peculiarities, from the movement of divine bodies to the way of behaving of liquids.

Differential math turned into a basic device for understanding and foreseeing regular cycles.

Gottfried Wilhelm Leibniz - The Introduction of Essential Analytics

At the same time, Gottfried Wilhelm Leibniz was autonomously creating necessary analytics, which supplements differential math and is similarly crucial in tackling genuine issues.

3.1 Leibniz's Initial Life and Schooling:

Leibniz, brought into the world on July 1, 1646, in Leipzig, Germany, showed a significant scholarly interest since early on. His different training in regulation and reasoning drove him to the investigation of science.

3.2 Minute Math and Documentation:

Leibniz presented a progressive documentation for math, including the necessary sign ($\int$) and the utilization of dx and dy to address tiny amounts. His methodology, known as "tiny analytics," zeroed in on the summation of imperceptibly little amounts to work out regions and take care of genuine issues.

3.3 Applications in Material science and Designing:

Leibniz's work on basic math tracked down prompt applications in material science and designing. Engineers utilized essential math to compute regions, volumes, and focuses of gravity, while physicists utilized it to comprehend complex actual peculiarities, for example, liquid elements and intensity stream.

Need of Analytics in Tackling Certifiable Issues

Math quickly acquired importance because of its imperative job in tending to a great many true issues across different fields.

4.1 Physical science and Mechanics:

In physical science, math turned into a crucial device for portraying the movement of items. Newton's laws of movement, formed utilizing differential math, gave the hypothetical establishment to mechanics, empowering exact expectations of planetary circles, shots, and other actual peculiarities.

4.2 Space science and Divine Mechanics:

Cosmologists utilized math to display the circles of planets and comets, foresee heavenly occasions, and refine the exactness of galactic perceptions. Analytics took into account the advancement of precise ephemerides, empowering the route of boats adrift and the investigation of unfamiliar regions.

4.3 Designing and Engineering:

Specialists and engineers outfit math to configuration structures, compute anxiety in materials, and enhance the states of scaffolds and structures. The investigation of analytics worked with the development of stupendous design accomplishments, like church buildings and extensions.

4.4 Financial aspects and Sociologies:

In the sociologies, math assumed a crucial part in demonstrating monetary frameworks, foreseeing populace development, and figuring out human conduct through numerical models. Analytics driven models gave significant bits of knowledge into the intricacies of human culture.

The Amalgamation of Differential and Necessary Math

As analytics kept on creating, mathematicians perceived the correlative idea of differential and essential analytics, prompting the combination of these two branches.

5.1 The Central Hypothesis of Math:

The central hypothesis of math, freely found by Newton and Leibniz, laid out a profound association among differential and basic analytics. This hypothesis takes into account the computation of regions and aggregations of amounts utilizing antiderivatives, overcoming any barrier between the two branches.

5.2 The Force of Speculation:

The blend of differential and fundamental math empowered mathematicians to sum up the standards of analytics to many capabilities and circumstances. This speculation extended the relevance of math to assorted fields of study.

1.2Historical figures who contributed to the groundwork for calculus, including Archimedes, Fermat, and Descartes.

The improvement of math in the late seventeenth century was a noteworthy numerical accomplishment, yet its underlying foundations can be followed back to the scholarly commitments of a few verifiable figures who laid the preparation for this progressive discipline. Among these trailblazers, Archimedes, Pierre de Fermat, and René Descartes stand apart for their earth shattering thoughts and basic ideas that made ready for the inevitable birth of analytics. In this investigation, we will dig into the lives and accomplishments of these prominent figures, revealing insight into their significant effect on the advancement of analytics.

Archimedes - The Old Trailblazer

1.1 Life and Foundation:

Archimedes of Syracuse, brought into the world in 287 BC in the Greek city-territory of Syracuse (presently in Italy), is eminent as quite possibly of the best mathematician, physicists, and designers of classical times. He hailed from a group of researchers and had major areas of strength for an establishment.

1.2 Commitments to Math Antecedents:

Archimedes made huge commitments to the advancement of analytics antecedents, especially with regards to math. His strategy for weariness, a method to compute regions and volumes of sporadic shapes by approximating them with less difficult mathematical figures, established the groundwork for the idea of cutoff points in math.

1.3 The Quadrature of the Parabola:

In his work "The Quadrature of the Parabola," Archimedes determined the region limited by an explanatory fragment and a straight line, spearheading the strategy for tracking down regions under bends — a focal idea in basic math.

Pierre de Fermat - The Dad of Current Number Hypothesis

2.1 Life and Foundation:

Pierre de Fermat, brought into the world in Beaumont-de-Lomagne, France, in 1601, was a legal counselor and novice mathematician. In spite of the fact that his essential calling lay in regulation, Fermat's numerical bits of knowledge established the groundwork for huge advancements in math.

2.2 Fermat's Strategy for Maxima and Minima:

Fermat's work on finding maxima and minima of bends, frequently viewed as a forerunner to math, involved researching properties of digressions to bends. He fostered a strategy for finding outrageous upsides of capabilities, which became fundamental in the later improvement of math.

2.3 Fermat's Guideline of Least Time:

Fermat's guideline of least time, a standard of optics, likewise assumed a part in the development of math. It stated that light follows the way of least time while going between two places, an idea with applications in math of varieties, a branch firmly connected with math.

René Descartes - The Dad of Insightful Calculation

3.1 Life and Foundation:

René Descartes, brought into the world in La Haye en Touraine, France, in 1596, was a logician, mathematician, and researcher. He is frequently alluded to as the "father of current way of thinking" and made huge commitments to science.

3.2 Insightful Math:

Descartes' momentous work in logical math, introduced in his "La Géométrie" (1637), presented addressing mathematical figures logarithmically. This development overcame any issues among variable based math and calculation, a pivotal step towards the improvement of math.

3.3 Direction Frameworks:

Descartes presented the Cartesian direction framework, which permitted mathematical shapes to be depicted utilizing arithmetical conditions. This framework reformed science and gave an incredible asset to taking care of mathematical issues, establishing the groundwork for later improvements in analytics.

The Union of Thoughts

4.1 Interaction of Thoughts:

The thoughts and commitments of Archimedes, Fermat, and Descartes were interconnected and impacted one another. Archimedes' strategy for weariness gave a mathematical way to deal with approximating regions, Fermat's work on maxima and minima managed improving bends, and Descartes' scientific calculation presented logarithmic portrayals of mathematical shapes.

4.2 Antecedents to Math:

Altogether, these authentic figures added to the fundamental components that would later develop into math. Archimedes' breaking point based strategies, Fermat's methods for tracking down outrageous qualities, and Descartes' logarithmic math all laid the preparation for the analytics of the seventeenth hundred years.

The Development of Math

5.1 Newton and Leibniz: The Introduction of Math:

The seventeenth century saw the finish of these forerunners in crafted by Isaac Newton and Gottfried Wilhelm Leibniz. Newton's "strategy for fluxions" and Leibniz's "minute math" united the ideas of cutoff points, subordinates, and integrals, making a brought together framework for grasping change and movement.

5.2 The Key Hypothesis of Math:

The combination of differential and vital analytics through the crucial hypothesis of math permitted mathematicians to sum up these thoughts and apply them to a large number of capabilities and issues. Math quickly developed into a strong numerical instrument for resolving certifiable issues.

1.3 The need for a systematic mathematical framework to describe change and motion.

Change and movement are central parts of the regular world, molding how we might interpret the universe. Whether it's the direction of a comet during that time sky, the development of a populace, or the speed increase of a moving vehicle, these peculiarities all include cycles of progress and movement. To understand and investigate these cycles really, humankind confronted the significant requirement for an orderly numerical system. This system, presently known as math, arose during the late seventeenth 100 years and upset the manner in which we depict, foresee, and control the elements of our general surroundings. In this investigation, we will dig into the verifiable and reasonable underpinnings of this need for an efficient numerical system to depict change and movement.

The Flightiness of Progress

1.1 Change as a Principal Peculiarity:

Change is universal in the regular world. It is seen in endless peculiarities, from the development of plants to the rot of radioactive materials. However, understanding and foreseeing these progressions ended up being really difficult for early masterminds.

1.2 Cosmology and Heavenly Mechanics:

Perceptions of divine bodies, like the planets and comets, brought up issues about the consistency of their movements. Early space experts wrestled with the inconsistencies and intricacies of heavenly circles, inciting the requirement for a methodical way to deal with portraying these movements.

1.3 The Flighty Universe:

Before the advancement of analytics, the normal world was frequently viewed as capricious and tumultuous. Occasions were noticed, however their basic standards remained covered in secret. To oversee this flightiness, a numerical system was earnestly required.

Archimedes and the Strategy for Weariness

2.1 Archimedes' Mathematical Understanding:

Archimedes of Syracuse, an old Greek mathematician and researcher, made spearheading commitments to grasping change and movement. His technique for weariness, created around 250 BC, addressed a critical stage towards an efficient numerical methodology.

2.2 Computing Regions and Volumes:

Archimedes' technique for depletion permitted him to surmised regions and volumes of unpredictable shapes and bodies by engraving them inside known mathematical figures. This technique gave a way to address the eccentricism of progress through mathematical thinking.

2.3 Cutoff Based Approaches:

Despite the fact that Archimedes' strategy was mathematical, it foreshadowed the breaking point based approaches that would become key to analytics. His utilization of ever-more modest mathematical shapes to surmised regions and volumes laid the basis for the idea of cutoff points in analytics.

The Requirement for Mathematical Portrayals

3.1 Variable based math's Job in Portraying Change:

While math offered significant bits of knowledge into the actual world, it was restricted in its capacity to depict complex and ceaselessly evolving processes. Polynomial math, with its emblematic portrayal of factors and conditions, arose as a correlative instrument to address this impediment.

3.2 The Renaissance and the Introduction of Arithmetical Request:

The Renaissance time frame saw a resurgence of interest in math and the improvement of variable based math. Researchers like François Viète and John Wallis started to utilize mathematical strategies to take care of issues recently handled with mathematical methods.

3.3 Descartes and Logical Calculation:

René Descartes, frequently thought to be the dad of logical math, presented the idea of addressing mathematical shapes logarithmically. His work, illustrated in "La Géométrie" (1637), associated polynomial math and calculation, giving an integral asset to depict change and movement.

Fermat and the Journey for Minima and Maxima

4.1 Fermat's Investigation of Limits:

Pierre de Fermat, a French legal counselor and mathematician of the seventeenth 100 years, looked to resolve inquiries of enhancement and limits in science. His work established the groundwork for tending to the elements of progress through the investigation of maxima and minima.

4.2 Fermat's Rule of Least Time:

Fermat's rule of least time in optics proposed that light follows the way of least time while going between two places. This idea, while not unequivocally math, involved improving an amount (time) and foreshadowed the analytics of varieties — a field intently attached to math.

The Blend of Techniques and the Introduction of Analytics

5.1 Newton and the Technique for Fluxions:

Isaac Newton, propelled by ancestors like Archimedes, Fermat, and Descartes, started to foster a methodical way to deal with portraying change and movement. His "technique for fluxions" presented the idea of the subsidiary, considering exact portrayals of paces of progress.

5.2 Leibniz and Little Analytics:

All the while, Gottfried Wilhelm Leibniz, affected by Fermat's work and Descartes' scientific strategies, created "minuscule math." Leibniz's work presented the basic, empowering the computation of collected change over the long haul.

5.3 The Introduction of Analytics:

The conversion of these endeavors by Newton and Leibniz finished in the introduction of analytics. Differential analytics, zeroed in on paces of progress and subsidiaries, and vital analytics, focused on collection and integrals, gave an orderly numerical structure to portray and foresee change and movement.

The Effect of Math on the World

6.1 Math as a General Language:

The improvement of math changed the manner in which we portray and grasp change and movement. It gave a general language to communicating normal peculiarities, from the movement of planets to the way of behaving of liquids.

6.2 Reforming Science and Designing:

Math turned into a key device in fields like physical science, designing, and financial matters. It permitted researchers and specialists to figure out exact models, foresee results, and plan imaginative answers for true issues.

6.3 The Consistently Extending Applications:

Over the long haul, math tracked down applications in different regions, including science, software engineering, and sociologies. Its flexibility and power keep on driving logical and mechanical progressions.

Chapter 2

Chapter 2

Newton's Method of Fluxions

Sir Isaac Newton's commitments to arithmetic and science are amazing, with one of his most huge accomplishments being the advancement of analytics. At the core of his work in analytics lies the "Technique for Fluxions." This imaginative methodology prepared for current differential math, upsetting the manner in which we comprehend and depict change and movement. In this thorough investigation, we will dive profound into Newton's life, the verifiable setting where he worked, and the complexities of his Strategy for Fluxions, which always changed the scene of math and science.

Isaac Newton - The Man Behind the Strategy

1.1 Early Life and Instruction:

Isaac Newton was brought into the world on January 4, 1643, in Woolsthorpe, Britain. He experienced childhood in a difficult climate, confronting neediness and familial misfortune at an early age. Regardless of these difficulties, he showed exceptional fitness for arithmetic and entered Trinity School, Cambridge, in 1661.

1.2 Scholarly Impacts:

Newton's time at Cambridge presented him to crafted by unmistakable mathematicians like René Descartes and John Wallis. These impacts assumed a vital part in profoundly shaping his numerical reasoning.

1.3 The Logical Upheaval:

The seventeenth century was set apart by the Logical Upheaval, a time of significant change in the manner in which people moved toward science and math. Newton arose as one of the focal figures of this scholarly development.

The Requirement for Another Numerical System

2.1 Change and Movement in the Regular World:

The regular world is described by change and movement, from the circles of planets to the way of behaving of falling items. Early masterminds attempted to foster a precise numerical system to comprehend and foresee these peculiarities.

2.2 Issues with Customary Math:

Calculation, the predominant numerical discipline of the time, was mismatched for portraying constantly evolving processes. Conventional mathematical strategies couldn't satisfactorily resolve questions including paces of progress.

2.3 The Journey for Another Arithmetic:

The requirement for a more flexible numerical structure to depict change and movement provoked mathematicians to investigate new techniques and thoughts. This mission established the groundwork for the advancement of math.

The Introduction of Differential Math

3.1 The Strategy for Fluxions Characterized:

Newton's Strategy for Fluxions was imagined during the 1660s. It planned to address the crucial ideas of movement, change, and rates. The expression "fluxion" alluded to the pace of progress of a variable.

3.2 Underpinnings of Differential Analytics:

At its center, differential math manages subsidiaries, which address paces of progress. Newton presented the idea of the subordinate as the restriction of the proportion of tiny changes in factors.

3.3 Documentation and Imagery:

Newton fostered a specific documentation for his Strategy for Fluxions, which included specks set over factors to show subsidiaries. This documentation, while particular from present day documentation, laid the foundation for ensuing advancements in analytics.

Standards of the Technique for Fluxions

4.1 Pace of Progress:

Key to the Technique for Fluxions is the idea of momentary pace of progress. Newton presented the possibility of a minute time span during which an amount goes through a microscopic change.

4.2 The Subordinate:

Newton's Strategy for Fluxions considered the computation of subsidiaries, addressing the pace of progress of a variable as for another variable. This idea was significant in taking care of issues connected with movement and change.

4.3 Digression Lines and Inclines:

Newton utilized his strategy to decide the incline of a bend at a particular point. This established the groundwork for understanding digression lines and gave a way to dissect the way of behaving of capabilities.

Utilizations of the Strategy for Fluxions

5.1 Heavenly Mechanics:

Newton applied his Strategy for Fluxions to divine mechanics, a field that had long perplexed space experts. He planned his laws of movement and all inclusive attraction utilizing differential math, empowering exact expectations of planetary circles.

5.2 Optics:

Newton's revenue in optics drove him to research the way of behaving of light and focal points. His Strategy for Fluxions permitted him to dissect the ways of light beams and determine the central standards of optics.

5.3 The Mechanical Way of thinking:

The Strategy for Fluxions assumed a critical part in propelling the mechanical way of thinking, a logical system that looked to make sense of normal peculiarities with regards to mechanical standards. This approach changed physical science and laid the basis for traditional mechanics.

The Leibniz-Newton Contention

6.1 The Development of Leibniz:

While Newton was fostering his Technique for Fluxions in Britain, Gottfried Wilhelm Leibniz, a German mathematician and thinker, was freely dealing with a comparable yet unmistakable arrangement of analytics in the late seventeenth hundred years.

6.2 Allegations of Copyright infringement:

The Leibniz-Newton debate emitted when the two mathematicians asserted credit for the creation of analytics. Allegations of counterfeiting and need questions stressed their relationship and isolated the numerical local area.

6.3 The Job of Documentation:

Integral to the discussion was the issue of documentation. Leibniz's documentation, which incorporated the necessary sign ($\int$) and the utilization of dx and dy, is nearer to present day documentation and turned out to be generally taken on.

The Tradition of Newton's Strategy for Fluxions

7.1 The Unification of Math and Material science:

Newton's Strategy for Fluxions reformed science as well as brought together it with the investigation of the actual world. His laws of movement and all inclusive attraction, figured out utilizing math, gave a thorough system to grasping the basic laws of the universe.

7.2 The Advancement of Math:

The Strategy for Fluxions, alongside Leibniz's math, established the groundwork for current analytics. The documentation and ideas acquainted by Newton go on with impact how math is instructed and applied today.

7.3 Effect on Science and Innovation:

Newton's commitments to math significantly affected science and innovation, empowering headways in physical science, designing, stargazing, and endless different fields. His work keeps on molding the manner in which we connect with the world.

2.1 Isaac Newton's early life, education, and scientific endeavors.

Isaac Newton, perhaps of the most persuasive figure throughout the entire existence of science and arithmetic, made a permanent imprint on human comprehension of the actual universe. His momentous work in mechanics, optics, arithmetic, and stargazing established the groundwork for present day science. To see the value in the extent of his accomplishments, it is fundamental to investigate his initial life, training, and the logical undertakings that impelled him to worldwide recognition.

The Early Existence of Isaac Newton

1.1 Birth and Youth:

Isaac Newton was conceived rashly on January 4, 1643, in Woolsthorpe, a little town in Lincolnshire, Britain. His introduction to the world came three months after the passing of his dad, likewise named Isaac Newton, a prosperous rancher. Youthful Isaac's initial years were set apart by private difficulties, including family insecurity and monetary hardships.

1.2 Instructive Starting points:

Newton went to Lord's School in Grantham, where he showed astounding fitness for learning. His scholarly ability and interest in the normal world started to arise during this period.

Instruction and Registration at Cambridge

2.1 The Cambridge Years:

In 1661, at 18 years old, Newton entered Trinity School, Cambridge, as a subsizar — a place that necessary him to perform modest errands in return for monetary help with his examinations. His time at Cambridge would shape his scholarly direction significantly.

2.2 Impact of Numerical Texts:

During his college years, Newton experienced crafted by compelling mathematicians like René Descartes and John Wallis. These texts touched off his enthusiasm for arithmetic, making way for his noteworthy commitments.

2.3 Numerical Virtuoso Arises:

While at Cambridge, Newton submerged himself in the investigation of arithmetic and started fostering his own imaginative thoughts. He immediately earned respect for his capacities, both as a mathematician and as a researcher.

Logical Undertakings and Accomplishments

3.1 Early Logical Commitments:

Newton's logical vocation started with examinations concerning different points, including optics, mechanics, and science. He fostered a standing for his uncommon abilities and inventive experiences.

3.2 The Reflecting Telescope:

Newton planned the principal functional reflecting telescope in 1668, a critical headway in cosmic perception. His telescope configuration reformed the field of optics and acquired him inescapable acknowledgment.

3.3 Laws of Movement:

In 1687, Newton distributed his amazing work, "Philosophiæ Naturalis Principia Mathematica" (Numerical Standards of Regular Way of thinking). This work of art spread out his three laws of movement, which structure the underpinning of traditional mechanics. The regulations portray the connection between the movement of an article and the powers following up on it.

3.4 General Attraction:

In a similar work, Newton presented the law of widespread attraction. He exhibited that each mass draws in each and every other mass through a power corresponding to the result of their masses and contrarily relative to the square of the distance between

them. This regulation gave an exhaustive clarification to heavenly movement and molded the field of cosmology.

Later Life and Scholarly Positions

4.1 Re-visitation of Cambridge:

Newton got back to Cambridge in 1667, where he was chosen an Individual of Trinity School. His arrangement as Lucasian Teacher of Math in 1669 denoted a lofty scholarly position, which he held for more than thirty years.

4.2 Struggle with Robert Hooke:

Newton's residency at Cambridge was not without discussion. He conflicted with Robert Hooke, an individual researcher, over their separate commitments to the comprehension of gravity and the laws of movement.

Inheritance and Effect

5.1 Numerical Commitments:

Newton's improvement of analytics, however damaged by the Leibniz-Newton need debate, altogether progressed arithmetic. His work on math laid the preparation for a deliberate way to deal with tackling issues of progress and movement.

5.2 Progressions in Optics:

Newton's spearheading work in optics uncovered the idea of light and variety, including the decay of white light into its constituent tones utilizing crystals. His examination significantly affected how we might interpret optics.

5.3 Progressive Laws of Movement:

Newton's laws of movement remain central in physical science, empowering exact computations of movement, the way of behaving of divine bodies, and designing applications. These regulations are vital to old style mechanics.

5.4 All inclusive Attractive energy and Stargazing:

Newton's law of all inclusive attractive energy changed cosmology, making sense of the circles of planets, the movement of heavenly bodies, and the way of behaving of comets. It laid the preparation for present day heavenly mechanics.

2.2In-depth exploration of Newton's method of "the calculus of fluents" or "fluxions."

Isaac Newton's numerical virtuoso rises above time, with his commitments to analytics remaining as a foundation of present day math. Among his spearheading works, "The

Math of Fluents" or "Fluxions" addresses a critical stage in the improvement of analytics. This thorough investigation digs profound into the complexities of Newton's "Fluxions," revealing insight into its authentic setting, standards, and the significant effect it has had on arithmetic and science.

The Verifiable Setting

1.1 The Requirement for Another Numerical Structure:

The seventeenth century was set apart by a developing acknowledgment of the requirement for an orderly numerical structure to address the difficulties presented by the investigation of progress and movement in the normal world. Traditional calculation and polynomial math were deficient to handle these mind boggling peculiarities.

1.2 The Test of Movement and Change:

The comprehension of peculiarities like planetary movement, falling items, and the direction of shots required new numerical apparatuses. The need to depict and break down ceaseless changes in amounts provoked mathematicians to look for imaginative arrangements.

1.3 The Antecedents to Math:

Mathematicians like Archimedes, Pierre de Fermat, and René Descartes had made huge commitments to the advancement of analytics forerunners. Newton's "Fluxions" addressed a finish of these early endeavors.

The Beginning of Fluxions

2.1 Newton's Numerical Foundation:

Isaac Newton's initial schooling at Cambridge College presented him to crafted by striking mathematicians and researchers. His interest with math, combined with his imaginative reasoning, set up for the advancement of "Fluxions."

2.2 Math Forerunners:

Prior to planning "Fluxions," Newton was affected by crafted by mathematicians like John Wallis, who had investigated thoughts connected with limitless series and the summation of regions under bends. These ideas assumed a vital part in the improvement of "Fluxions."

2.3 Advancements in Documentation:

Newton acquainted another documentation framework with address his numerical thoughts. He utilized dabs above letters to demonstrate subordinates, a documentation that would later develop into the recognizable images for separation in current math.

Standards of Fluxions

3.1 Microscopic Changes:

The center idea of "Fluxions" spun around minute changes. Newton considered amounts that shift ceaselessly, and he looked to comprehend how these amounts change at explicit moments or space.

3.2 Pace of Progress:

Newton's "Fluxions" planned to compute the pace of progress of an amount at a given moment. This idea is comparable to the cutting edge subsidiary, addressing the slant of a bend at a solitary point.

3.3 The Subordinate and the Fluxion:

Newton's numerical developments incorporated the presentation of the subsidiary as the "first fluents" and the "second fluents," which compared to the first and second subordinates, separately.

Uses of Fluxions

4.1 Newton's Laws of Movement:

Newton applied his "Fluxions" to determine his renowned laws of movement. These regulations established the groundwork for old style mechanics and gave a precise system to grasping the elements of actual items.

4.2 All inclusive Attraction:

Newton's "Fluxions" assumed a focal part in the improvement of his law of general attraction. He utilized the idea of momentary paces of progress to make sense of the movement of divine bodies and their gravitational cooperations.

4.3 Optics and Variety Hypothesis:

In the field of optics, Newton's "Fluxions" permitted him to explore the way of behaving of light and variety. His work on scattering, the deterioration of light, and variety hypothesis were instrumental in propelling comprehension we might interpret optics.

The Development of Fluxions into Present day Math

5.1 The Leibniz-Newton Need Debate:

The advancement of analytics was set apart by the popular Leibniz-Newton need debate. Gottfried Wilhelm Leibniz, freely of Newton, likewise created math, utilizing an alternate documentation framework. The contention prompted critical pressures between the two mathematicians.

5.2 The Development of Current Documentation:

Regardless of the debate, math developed as a bound together field, incorporating the thoughts of both Newton and Leibniz. Present day documentation, with images, for example, dx and dy, slowly supplanted the first "Fluxions" documentation.

5.3 Math as a Bringing together Numerical Structure:

The combination of Newton's "Fluxions" and Leibniz's math brought about an extensive numerical structure. This unification permitted mathematicians to address a variety of issues connected with change, movement, and progression.

2.3 Newton's mathematical innovations, including the Fundamental Theorem of Calculus.

Isaac Newton, a transcending figure throughout the entire existence of science and math, made a permanent imprint on human comprehension with his weighty commitments. Among his numerous numerical developments, the Basic Hypothesis of Math remains as a foundation of present day analytics. In this exhaustive investigation, we will dig into Newton's numerical advancements, zeroing in on his work in fostering the Essential Hypothesis of Analytics and its significant effect on arithmetic and science.

Newton's Numerical Foundation

1.1 Early Numerical Ability:

Since the beginning, Isaac Newton showed an inborn ability for science. His numerical excursion started at Cambridge College, where he fostered an interest for the subject.

1.2 Impacts and Ancestors:

Newton's work was affected by noticeable mathematicians and researchers of his time, including John Wallis and Johannes Kepler. These impacts assumed a urgent part in shaping his numerical reasoning.

The Requirement for Analytics

2.1 Difficulties in Science:

The seventeenth century presented significant difficulties in understanding and depicting normal peculiarities including change and movement. Traditional calculation and variable based math were inappropriate to deal with the intricacies of consistently evolving amounts.

2.2 Development of Analytics Forerunners:

Mathematicians like Archimedes, Pierre de Fermat, René Descartes, and John Wallis made critical commitments to the improvement of analytics antecedents. These early endeavors laid the basis for Newton's advancements.

Newton's Advancement of Analytics

3.1 Tiny Math:

Newton's "Fluxions," as he called them, addressed a spearheading way to deal with math. He presented the idea of microscopic changes to figure out the momentary paces of progress of amounts.

3.2 Pace of Progress:

A central part of Newton's math was the assurance of immediate paces of progress. He perceived the significance of understanding how amounts change at explicit moments or space.

3.3 The Subsidiary:

Newton's numerical developments incorporated the presentation of the subordinate as a way to address the pace of progress of a capability. His thoughts established the groundwork for differential math.

The Major Hypothesis of Math

4.1 Reasonable Outline:

The Essential Hypothesis of Math is a foundation of analytics, connecting the ideas of separation and mix. That's what it expresses in the event that a capability is nonstop on a shut stretch, its basic can be determined utilizing antiderivatives of the capability.

4.2 Newton's Commitments:

Newton's work on the Major Hypothesis of Math was instrumental in the advancement of vital analytics. He laid out the connection among incorporation and separation, giving an orderly way to deal with working out regions under bends.

4.3 The Job of Antiderivatives:

How Newton might interpret antiderivatives was urgent to the Key Hypothesis of Math. He perceived that the opposite course of separation — tracking down the first capability from its subordinate — was fundamental to vital math.

The Effect of the Major Hypothesis of Math

5.1 Numerical Progressions:

The Crucial Hypothesis of Analytics upset math. It gave a bringing together system that overcame any issues among separation and mix, permitting mathematicians to handle complex issues in different fields.

5.2 Applications in Science:

The hypothesis' application reached out a long ways past science. It assumed a pivotal part in the improvement of physical science, designing, financial matters, and different sciences, empowering exact displaying and examination of dynamic frameworks.

5.3 Current Analytics:

The Basic Hypothesis of Analytics, alongside crafted by counterparts like Gottfried Wilhelm Leibniz, added to the development of current math. Today, it is a fundamental part of each and every math educational program.

Newton's Heritage in Arithmetic and Science

6.1 The Unification of Arithmetic:

Newton's numerical advancements, including the Key Hypothesis of Analytics, brought together already unique areas of arithmetic. His work established the groundwork for the precise investigation of progress and movement.

6.2 Headways in Science:

Newton's commitments to analytics and his laws of movement changed science. His numerical system empowered the exact investigation of actual peculiarities and the definition of hypotheses that depict the regular world.

6.3 A Demonstration of Human Resourcefulness:

Newton's numerical developments act as a demonstration of the force of human idea and development. His investigation of analytics and the Major Hypothesis keeps on moving mathematicians, researchers, and scholars to test the secrets of the universe.

Chapter 3

Chapter 3

Leibniz's Infinitesimal Calculus

Gottfried Wilhelm Leibniz, a polymath of the seventeenth 100 years, left a persevering through heritage in math through his improvement of little math. This part of math reformed the manner in which we comprehend and control consistently evolving amounts, establishing the groundwork for current analytics. In this thorough investigation, we will dig into Leibniz's life, the authentic setting in which he worked, and the complexities of his tiny analytics, which perpetually changed the scene of arithmetic and science.

Gottfried Wilhelm Leibniz - The Man Behind the Analytics

1.1 Early Life and Training:

Gottfried Wilhelm Leibniz was brought into the world on July 1, 1646, in Leipzig, Germany. Since early on, he showed enormous scholarly gifts. He sought after a different scope of interests, including math, reasoning, and regulation, all through his life.

1.2 The Library and Correspondence:

Leibniz's work benefited extraordinarily from his admittance to broad libraries and his broad correspondence with noticeable researchers across Europe. His capacity to team up and trade thoughts was instrumental in the advancement of his math.

1.3 Way of thinking and Power:

Leibniz's philosophical investigations into the idea of the real world and power impacted his numerical reasoning. His ideas of "monads" and the "rule of adequate explanation" assumed a part in his way to deal with math.

The Requirement for Math

2.1 Difficulties in Science:

The seventeenth century saw a developing requirement for a numerical structure to address the intricacies of progress and movement. Customary math, in light of calculation and polynomial math, battled to deal with persistently evolving amounts.

2.2 The Issue of Digressions:

Math had its underlying foundations in issues connected with digressions, regions, and paces of progress. Mathematicians looked for answers for these issues, and Leibniz was at the very front of creating inventive techniques.

2.3 Antecedents to Math:

Early mathematicians like Archimedes, Pierre de Fermat, René Descartes, and John Wallis added to the advancement of analytics antecedents. Their thoughts gave the foundation whereupon Leibniz would construct.

The Introduction of Minuscule Math

3.1 Infinitesimals and the Differential Math:

Leibniz presented the idea of infinitesimals, or "boundlessly little" amounts, as the premise of his differential math. He perceived that these amounts could be utilized to grasp change and paces of progress.

3.2 Groundworks of Differential Math:

At the core of Leibniz's minute math was the possibility of the subordinate. He fostered a documentation framework, including the recognizable "d" for differentials, which considered exact computations of subsidiaries and paces of progress.

Standards of Little Math

4.1 The Idea of the Subsidiary:

Leibniz's analytics meant to compute momentary paces of progress. He presented the subordinate as a central idea, catching the incline of a bend at a particular point.

4.2 The Item Rule and Chain Rule:

Leibniz fostered the item rule and the chain rule, fundamental apparatuses in math for separating composite capabilities and results of capabilities. These standards altogether extended the pertinence of analytics.

The Fundamental Analytics

5.1 The Vital as Aggregation:

Leibniz stretched out his math to foster the fundamental analytics. He considered the indispensable to be a method for gathering amounts over a span, resolving issues connected with regions and summation.

5.2 Documentation and the Fundamental Sign:

Leibniz's documentation for the fundamental, which incorporated the vital sign ($\int$) and the utilization of dx and dy, is nearer to current documentation. His emblematic portrayal made it more straightforward to work with and grasp integrals.

The Leibniz-Newton Need Question

6.1 Equal Turns of events:

All the while with Leibniz's work, Isaac Newton was fostering his own analytics. The free however equal improvements of math by Leibniz and Newton ignited a need debate that would endure for a really long time.

6.2 The Job of Documentation:

Fundamental to the debate was the distinction in documentation and language among Leibniz's and Newton's methodologies. Leibniz's more present day and natural documentation prompted its boundless reception.

The Effect of Minuscule Math

7.1 Numerical Progressions:

Leibniz's microscopic math gave an orderly structure to tackling issues including consistent change. It assumed a focal part in the improvement of science, considering exact estimations in different fields.

7.2 Applications in Science and Designing:

Minuscule analytics tracked down applications in physical science, designing, stargazing, and endless other logical disciplines. It empowered the detailing of exact models, forecasts, and mechanical headways.

7.3 Current Analytics:

Leibniz's microscopic analytics, alongside Newton's commitments, established the groundwork for present day math. The standards and documentation acquainted by Leibniz go on with shape how math is educated and applied today.

3.1 Gottfried Wilhelm Leibniz's background, influences, and intellectual pursuits.

Gottfried Wilhelm Leibniz, a polymath of the seventeenth and eighteenth hundreds of years, was quite possibly of the most persuasive mastermind throughout the entire existence of Western way of thinking, math, and science. His boundless scholarly pursuits made a permanent imprint on different disciplines, from math and reasoning to

regulation and discretion. In this thorough investigation, we will dig into Leibniz's experience, his assorted impacts, and his complex scholarly excursion.

The Early Existence of Gottfried Wilhelm Leibniz

1.1 Birth and Family:

Gottfried Wilhelm Leibniz was brought into the world on July 1, 1646, in Leipzig, Germany, to Friedrich Leibniz, a teacher of moral way of thinking, and Catharina Sucker, the little girl of a noticeable legal counselor. His family's experience in scholastics and regulation would impact his future interests.

1.2 Training and Early Interests:

Leibniz accepted his initial training in Leipzig and went to the Nicolai School. His initial advantages spread over many subjects, including works of art, reasoning, and regulation.

1.3 Impact of Books and Libraries:

Leibniz's openness to broad libraries, including his dad's assortment, encouraged his energy for perusing and investigation. These libraries gave him admittance to an immense store of information, forming his scholarly turn of events.

The Scholarly Milieu of seventeenth Century Europe

2.1 The Logical Upset:

The seventeenth century was set apart by the Logical Upset, a time of significant change in the manner in which Europeans moved toward science, math, and reasoning. The scholarly climate of the time would influence Leibniz's reasoning.

2.2 Renaissance Humanism:

Leibniz was impacted by Renaissance humanism, which underscored the significance of information and the possibility that people could make huge scholarly commitments.

2.3 Philosophical Ways of thinking:

The predominant philosophical discussions of the time, including those among experimentation and logic, would illuminate Leibniz's philosophical positions.

Leibniz's Assorted Scholarly Pursuits

3.1 Way of thinking:

Leibniz is maybe most popular for his philosophical commitments, including his way of thinking of monads, the rule of adequate explanation, and his hopefulness about the

"best of every single imaginable world." His magical requests reshaped the field of reasoning.

3.2 Science:

Leibniz's numerical work was weighty. He freely created little math, presented emblematic documentation, and made huge commitments to the field of polynomial math and combinatorics.

3.3 Regulation and Discretion:

Notwithstanding his scholarly interests, Leibniz stood firm on footholds in regulation and discretion. His lawful mastery and strategic abilities were utilized in different limits, including work for the Balloter of Mainz and the Hanoverian court.

3.4 Language and Etymology:

Leibniz had a profound interest in language and semantics. He proposed the possibility of a widespread language and fostered the idea of a parallel numeral framework, which would later become essential in figuring.

Compelling Figures in Leibniz's Day to day existence

4.1 Jakob Thomasius:

Jakob Thomasius, a family companion and teacher of regulation, assumed a critical part in Leibniz's initial training and openness to different scholarly disciplines.

4.2 Bartholomaeus Keckermann:

Leibniz concentrated under Bartholomaeus Keckermann, an eminent thinker, whose lessons impacted his initial philosophical turn of events.

4.3 Christiaan Huygens:

Leibniz compared with Christiaan Huygens, a Dutch mathematician and physicist, on subjects connected with science and physical science. Their trade of thoughts significantly affected Leibniz's work.

Leibniz's Heritage and Effect

5.1 Math and Science:

Leibniz's commitments to math, especially the improvement of analytics and emblematic documentation, keep on molding the field today. His work established the groundwork for present day math and physical science.

5.2 Way of thinking:

Leibniz's way of thinking, however bantered during his lifetime, lastingly affects power, epistemology, and morals. His thoughts on the idea of the real world, pre-laid out congruity, and the standard of adequate explanation remain subjects of philosophical request.

5.3 Language and Registering:

Leibniz's ideas in etymology and the double numeral framework are fundamental to the advancement of current processing and data hypothesis.

3.2Leibniz's development of the "calculus" using notation based on differentials and infinitesimals.

Gottfried Wilhelm Leibniz, a polymath of the seventeenth hundred years, made noteworthy commitments to science through the improvement of math. Not at all like his contemporary Isaac Newton, Leibniz presented an original documentation framework in light of differentials and infinitesimals, which essentially progressed the field. In this thorough investigation, we will dive into Leibniz's progressive way to deal with analytics, his remarkable documentation, and the getting through effect of his commitments on math and science.

The Setting of Numerical Difficulties in the seventeenth 100 years

1.1 The Requirement for Analytics:

The seventeenth century saw a developing requirement for a numerical system that could resolve issues including consistent change, movement, and paces of progress. Customary numerical techniques in view of math and polynomial math demonstrated deficient for these mind boggling difficulties.

1.2 The Issue of Digressions:

Math had its beginnings in issues connected with digressions, regions, and bends. Mathematicians looked for answers for these issues, establishing the groundwork for the advancement of analytics.

Leibniz's Numerical Foundation and Early Impacts

2.1 Early Instruction and Impacts:

Leibniz's initial schooling in Leipzig and his openness to researchers and libraries gave a strong groundwork to his future numerical pursuits. He was impacted by crafted by noticeable mathematicians and researchers of his time.

2.2 Impact of Jakob Thomasius:

Leibniz's relationship with Jakob Thomasius, a family companion and teacher of regulation, acquainted him with different scholastic trains and sustained his scholarly interest.

Leibniz's Little Math

3.1 Infinitesimals and Differentials:

Leibniz presented the idea of infinitesimals — limitlessly little amounts — as the premise of his analytics. He created differentials, addressed by images like dx and dy, to indicate these minute changes.

3.2 Underpinnings of Differential Analytics:

At the center of Leibniz's math was the possibility of separation. He presented an orderly technique for computing subsidiaries, which addressed paces of progress and inclines of bends.

Standards of Leibniz's Analytics

4.1 The Differential as a Restricting Interaction:

Leibniz saw differentials as a restriction of the proportion of little changes. This approach permitted him to work out momentary paces of progress and catch the way of behaving of persistently fluctuating amounts.

4.2 Documentation and Imagery:

One of Leibniz's most huge advancements was his emblematic documentation for math. He utilized images like dy, dx, and $\int$ (vital sign) to address differentials, subordinates, and integrals, making complex estimations more natural.

The Essential Hypothesis of Analytics in Leibniz's Structure

5.1 Calculated Outline:

Leibniz's differential and vital analytics finished in his detailing of the Basic Hypothesis of Math. This hypothesis laid out a significant association among separation and combination.

5.2 The Job of Antiderivatives:

Leibniz perceived the significance of antiderivatives — capabilities whose subsidiaries match a given capability — in the Principal Hypothesis. He presented the idea of endless integrals to address antiderivatives.

Applications and Effect of Leibniz's Analytics

6.1 Numerical Headways:

Leibniz's analytics documentation and ideas upset arithmetic. His work gave an orderly structure to taking care of issues connected with change, movement, and consistent variety.

6.2 Logical and Designing Applications:

Leibniz's analytics tracked down applications in different logical disciplines, including physical science, designing, stargazing, and financial matters. It empowered the exact displaying of dynamic frameworks and the plan of regulations administering regular peculiarities.

6.3 Current Math:

Leibniz's differential and vital math, alongside his documentation, established the groundwork for present day analytics. His commitments keep on molding how analytics is educated and applied in contemporary math and science.

3.3 A comparison of Leibniz's and Newton's notations and approaches to calculus.

The advancement of analytics in the late seventeenth century is quite possibly of the main achievement throughout the entire existence of science. Two of the most conspicuous figures in this advancement were Gottfried Wilhelm Leibniz and Sir Isaac Newton. While both Leibniz and Newton autonomously designed math, they did so utilizing various documentations and approaches. This paper will investigate and analyze the documentations and approaches of Leibniz and Newton to analytics, featuring their likenesses and contrasts and looking at the effect of their work on the field of math.

Leibniz's Documentation and Approach

Gottfried Wilhelm Leibniz, a German mathematician and scholar, is known for his imaginative documentation in math. His documentation is portrayed by the utilization of images, for example, 'd' for separation and '∫' for incorporation, which are still broadly utilized today. Leibniz's way to deal with math depended on the idea of infinitesimals, which are amounts that are boundlessly little however not equivalent to nothing.

One of the critical parts of Leibniz's documentation is the utilization of differentials. He presented the documentation dy/dx to address the subordinate of a capability y regarding x. This documentation made it simple to communicate and control subordinates and integrals. Leibniz's documentation underlined the possibility that

separation and joining were converse tasks, as addressed by the key hypothesis of math.

Leibniz's way to deal with math likewise underscored the significance of mathematical instinct. He frequently utilized mathematical charts and visual thinking to make sense of numerical ideas. This mathematical viewpoint helped understudies and mathematicians of his opportunity to all the more likely figure out the standards of analytics.

One more significant commitment of Leibniz was his documentation for higher-request subordinates. He presented the documentation d^2y/dx^2 for the subsequent subordinate, d^3y/dx^3 for the third subsidiary, etc. This documentation made it more straightforward to work with higher-request subsidiaries and prepared for the improvement of differential conditions.

Newton's Documentation and Approach

Sir Isaac Newton, an English mathematician and physicist, fostered his own way to deal with analytics autonomously of Leibniz. Newton's documentation and way to deal with analytics depended on the idea of fluxions, which were paces of progress. Not at all like Leibniz's documentation, which utilized differentials, Newton's documentation utilized the spot documentation.

In Newton's documentation, the subordinate of a capability y concerning time t was addressed as $\dot{y}$ (articulated as "y-dab"). Essentially, the subsequent subsidiary was addressed as $\ddot{y}$ (articulated as "y-twofold dab"). While this documentation might show up less natural than Leibniz's, it filled its need in Newton's mathematical way to deal with analytics.

Newton's way to deal with math included considering amounts as shifting ceaselessly with time. He saw movement as the crucial idea and applied math to depict changes moving. Newton's work in analytics was firmly associated with his laws of movement and the law of general attraction.

One of Newton's huge commitments was the improvement of the strategy for fluxions, which was an antecedent to the cutting edge idea of cutoff points. He involved the possibility of a minuscule change in a variable to work out subsidiaries and integrals. While his methodology was thoughtfully not quite the same as Leibniz's, it yielded comparable outcomes and added to the improvement of math.

Examination of Documentations and Approaches
Documentations:

Leibniz's documentation is broadly perceived and utilized in present day analytics. It gives a natural method for communicating subordinates and integrals, making it open to understudies and mathematicians.

Newton's speck documentation, then again, is less regularly utilized today. It might show up less natural, particularly to fledglings, however it filled its need with regards to Newton's mathematical methodology.

Way to deal with Infinitesimals:

Leibniz's methodology depended on infinitesimals, which were amounts that could be treated as genuine numbers however were imperceptibly little. This approach was basic to the advancement of the thorough epsilon-delta meaning of cutoff points.

Newton's methodology utilized fluxions, which were paces of progress over imperceptibly modest spans. While this approach worked successfully, it was less worried about the primary issues of math that Leibniz's methodology tended to.

Mathematical versus Kinematic:

Leibniz's methodology had major areas of strength for an accentuation, zeroing in on the mathematical translation of subordinates and integrals. This made it open to those with a mathematical instinct.

Newton's methodology was more kinematic, underlining the investigation of movement and change. His laws of movement and the law of widespread attraction were intently attached to his analytics work.

Higher-Request Subordinates:

Leibniz's documentation for higher-request subsidiaries (d^2y/dx^2, d^3y/dx^3, and so on) was direct and became standard documentation in math.

Newton's documentation for higher-request subsidiaries was less normalized and not as broadly took on.

Inheritance and Effect

Both Leibniz and Newton made significant commitments to the advancement of analytics, and their documentations and approaches keep on impacting the field of science right up 'til now.

Leibniz's documentation, with its emphasis on differentials and mathematical instinct, stays a foundation of analytics training. His documentation is instrumental in taking care of issues across different logical and designing disciplines, and the idea of the necessary sign (∫) is all around perceived.

Newton's way to deal with analytics, with its accentuation on movement and change, laid the preparation for current physical science and designing. While his speck documentation is less normally utilized, his thoughts regarding paces of progress and

the idea of cutoff points were instrumental in the improvement of analytics as a thorough numerical discipline.

Eventually, the Leibniz-Newton math need debate, which emerged because of the free improvement of math by the two mathematicians, fills in as a demonstration of the meaning of their work. Today, analytics is educated and worked on utilizing a mix of Leibniz's and Newton's documentations, mirroring the rich history and getting through effect of these two wonderful mathematicians.

Chapter 4

The Priority Dispute Begins

The seventeenth century was a noteworthy period throughout the entire existence of science, set apart by the rise of weighty thoughts and the commitments of splendid mathematicians. One of the main improvements during this time was the innovation of math. Notwithstanding, the introduction of analytics was joined by a wild and getting through need question between two goliaths of science: Gottfried Wilhelm Leibniz and Sir Isaac Newton. This debate, known as the "Math Need Question," rotated around the subject of who originally imagined analytics and who merited recognition for its creation. This exposition dives into the beginnings, key occasions, and enduring effect of the need question, revealing insight into the perplexing connection among Leibniz and Newton and their commitments to the field of science.

Foundation: The Development of Analytics

Prior to digging into the need question, understanding the authentic setting and the scholarly environment that made ready for the advancement of calculus is fundamental.

1.1 Ancestors and Forerunners

Arithmetic had been advancing for a really long time, with key commitments from old Greek mathematicians like Euclid and Archimedes.

The requirement for better instruments for managing issues connected with movement, change, and bends prompted the advancement of techniques, for example, the strategy for depletion and the strategy for indivisibles.

Mathematicians like John Wallis, Pierre de Fermat, and Bonaventura Cavalieri gained critical headway in fostering these techniques, laying the basis for analytics.

1.2 Inspiration for Math

By the seventeenth hundred years, there was a developing interest for numerical procedures to dissect and tackle issues in material science, stargazing, designing, and different fields.

Math arose as a reaction to these requests, giving a brought together system to figuring out change, paces of progress, and bends.

The Contention Starts: Leibniz and Newton

The need question can be followed back to the free and almost synchronous improvement of math by Leibniz and Newton. The two mathematicians carried extraordinary points of view and documentations to the field, which in the long run prompted disarray and pressure.

2.1 Leibniz's Commitment

Gottfried Wilhelm Leibniz, a German mathematician and logician, fostered his rendition of math in the last part of the 1670s.

Leibniz's documentation, portrayed by images like 'd' for separation and '∫' for mix, was a significant advancement that incredibly worked with the review and utilization of math.

His methodology depended on the idea of infinitesimals — amounts that are boundlessly little however not equivalent to nothing. Leibniz accepted that math could be grounded in this idea.

2.2 Newton's Commitment

Sir Isaac Newton, an English mathematician and physicist, freely fostered his own form of analytics around a similar time as Leibniz.

Newton's methodology, as opposed to Leibniz's, depended on the idea of fluxions — paces of progress.

He utilized his math to concentrate on movement, establishing the groundwork for his laws of movement and the law of general attraction.

Distribution of Numerical Works

The need question raised with the distribution of Leibniz's and Newton's numerical works, which uncovered their separate documentations and approaches.

3.1 Leibniz's Distributions

Leibniz's most memorable distribution on math, "Nova Methodus star Maximis et Minimis," showed up in Acta Eruditorum in 1684. This work presented his documentations and standards.

Leibniz kept on distributing on analytics, setting his documentation and approach, and making sense of how tackling different numerical and actual problems could be utilized.

3.2 Newton's Distributions

Newton's earliest work on math stayed unpublished during his lifetime. Be that as it may, he imparted his plans to a select gathering of mathematicians, like Isaac Hand truck and John Collins.

In 1693, Newton's technique for fluxions was distributed post mortem in the "Strategy for Fluxions," altered by John Colson. This work gave experiences into Newton's way to deal with analytics.

The Question Heightens

As Leibniz and Newton earned respect for their commitments to math, the stage was set for a disagreement regarding need and credit.

4.1 Letters and Correspondence

The question started with a progression of letters traded between mathematicians, researchers, and scholars, including Leibniz, Newton, John Collins, and Henry Oldenburg.

In one letter to Collins dated June 21, 1677, Newton shared his strategy for fluxions, demonstrating that he had been dealing with analytics for quite a long time.

Leibniz related with a few people, including Oldenburg, sharing his thoughts on math, however without uncovering the subtleties of his documentation.

4.2 Allegations and Counter-Allegations

The question heightened when both Leibniz and Newton started blaming each other for counterfeiting and guaranteeing need in the creation of analytics.

Newton blamed Leibniz for having taken his thoughts, refering to his 1677 letter to Collins as proof. He professed to have imagined analytics years before Leibniz's work.

Leibniz shielded his autonomous innovation, contending that his documentation and standards were unmistakable from Newton's and that he had created analytics without information on Newton's work.

4.3 Contribution of the Illustrious Society

The Illustrious Society of London became entangled in the question, as it had individuals who were steady of both Newton and Leibniz.

The General public led examinations and consultations to decide the need of analytics, which further powered the discussion.

The Fallout and Heritage

The need question had enduring ramifications for the notorieties of Leibniz and Newton and for the improvement of analytics as a field of science.

5.1 Effect on Successors

In spite of the sharpness of the question, both Leibniz's and Newton's documentations and approaches contributed altogether to the improvement of math.

Leibniz's documentation stays crucial to present day analytics, while Newton's strategies gave important bits of knowledge into the investigation of movement and change.

5.2 Acknowledgment and Authentic Appraisal

The debate finished without a reasonable goal, and both Leibniz and Newton are presently perceived as free prime supporters of math.

Students of history of arithmetic recognize the peculiarity of their commitments and note that they moved toward math according to alternate points of view and with various documentations.

5.3 Enduring Effect

The need question among Leibniz and Newton fills in as a useful example throughout the entire existence of science and math, featuring the significance of clear correspondence, legitimate attribution, and joint effort.

The advancement of analytics, in spite of the debate, reformed math and had sweeping ramifications for science, designing, and innovation.

4.1 The emergence of accusations of plagiarism and priority between Newton and Leibniz.

The rise of allegations of counterfeiting and need between Sir Isaac Newton and Gottfried Wilhelm Leibniz in the improvement of math is a crucial section throughout the entire existence of science. This debate, which unfurled in the late seventeenth hundred years, rotated around the subject of who had the legitimate case to the creation of analytics. This article investigates the occasions paving the way to the allegations, the contentions made by the two sides, and the enduring effect of this question on the tradition of these two numerical goliaths.

Early Correspondence and Sharing of Thoughts

The seeds of the need debate were planted in the early correspondence between Newton, Leibniz, and different mathematicians of their time. It is fundamental to comprehend the setting of their communications to get a handle on the movement of the debate.

1.1 Newton's Initial Correspondence

Newton had fostered his own form of math, which he alluded to as the "strategy for fluxions," by the mid-1670s.

In a letter dated June 21, 1677, Newton kept in touch with John Collins, a mathematician and individual of the Illustrious Society, illustrating the essential

standards of his analytics. He sent Collins a duplicate of his work named "De Analysi per Aequationes Numero Terminorum Infinitas" (On Investigation by Limitless Series).

1.2 Leibniz's Correspondence

Leibniz, who had freely fostered his analytics, started comparing with English mathematicians and researchers in the last part of the 1670s.

Leibniz traded letters with figures like Henry Oldenburg, Secretary of the Regal Society, and John Wallis, examining numerical thoughts without uncovering the particulars of his documentation or approach.

Newton's Allegation

The debate heightened when Newton blamed Leibniz for copyright infringement, declaring that Leibniz had duplicated his thoughts and techniques.

2.1 Newton's Allegation of Copyright infringement

Newton's allegation originated from his conviction that Leibniz had taken his thoughts, especially those illustrated in his letter to John Collins.

Newton contended that his technique for fluxions was created a long time before Leibniz's work and that Leibniz's documentation and standards firmly looked like his own.

2.2 Newton's Letter to the Imperial Society

In June 1712, Newton composed a letter to the Imperial Society specifying his allegations against Leibniz. This letter became known as the "Commercium Epistolicum."

Newton introduced a timetable of occasions, underscoring his initial work on math and the supposed similitudes among his and Leibniz's documentations and techniques.

Leibniz's Protection

Gottfried Wilhelm Leibniz answered Newton's allegations with an enthusiastic protection of his free development of math.

3.1 Leibniz's Case of Autonomy

Leibniz passionately prevented Newton's claims from getting copyright infringement. He stated that he had created math autonomously and without information on Newton's work.

Leibniz stressed that his documentation and standards were unmistakable from Newton's and contended that any likenesses were because of the normal combination of numerical thoughts.

3.2 Leibniz's Letter to the Regal Society

Leibniz composed a letter to the Regal Society in September 1712, answering Newton's allegations. This letter is frequently alluded to as the "Supplement to the Commercium Epistolicum."

In his letter, Leibniz safeguarded his documentation and his methodology, making sense of how he had shown up at his math freely.

The Job of the Imperial Society

The Imperial Society of London assumed a focal part in intervening the question among Newton and Leibniz.

4.1 The Regal Society's Examination

The Regal Society viewed the allegations in a serious way and sent off an examination to decide the need of math.

The examination included checking on records, letters, and declarations from mathematicians who had related with both Newton and Leibniz.

4.2 Blended Gathering

The Regal Society's examination didn't give a reasonable decision for one or the other

Newton or Leibniz.

A few individuals from the Regal Society, including the people who were thoughtful to Newton, leaned toward his case, while others had confidence in Leibniz's freedom.

Inheritance and Verifiable Evaluation

The allegations of copyright infringement and need among Newton and Leibniz had expansive ramifications for the tradition of the two mathematicians and for the improvement of analytics.

5.1 Acknowledgment of The two Mathematicians

In spite of the discussion and waiting questions, both Newton and Leibniz are presently perceived as autonomous fellow benefactors of math.

Antiquarians of arithmetic recognize the peculiarity of their commitments, the distinctions in their documentations and approaches, and the concurrent advancement of math in Britain and mainland Europe.

5.2 Effect on Cooperation and Attribution

The need question fills in as a wake up call throughout the entire existence of science and math, featuring the significance of clear correspondence, legitimate attribution, and joint effort among researchers.

5.3 Persevering through Effect of Documentations

The documentations and approaches created by both Newton and Leibniz keep on molding the review and practice of math.

Leibniz's documentation, portrayed by images like 'd' for separation and '∫' for joining,

stays a crucial piece of present day math.

5.4 The Impact of the Debate

The debate lastingly affected the connection among English and mainland European mathematicians, adding to pressures in the numerical local area.

4.2 Correspondence and publications that fueled the controversy.

The Newton-Leibniz need debate, a critical episode throughout the entire existence of science, was powered fundamentally by correspondence and distributions. This quarrel, which rotated around the innovation of analytics, pitted two numerical monsters, Sir Isaac Newton and Gottfried Wilhelm Leibniz, against one another. Their letters and compositions give significant experiences into the development of the discussion and the contentions made by the two sides. This paper investigates the critical correspondence and distributions that assumed a focal part in escalating the question.

Newton's Letter to John Collins (1677)

The Newton-Leibniz need debate follows its beginnings back to a letter composed by Isaac Newton to John Collins, a mathematician and individual of the Illustrious Society.

1.1 Substance of the Letter

In his letter to Collins, dated June 21, 1677, Newton framed the crucial standards of his math, which he alluded to as the "technique for fluxions."

He presented the idea of fluxions (paces of progress) and made sense of how these ideas could be utilized to track down digressions to bends and decide maxima and minima.

Newton likewise gave an illustration of the strategy applied to taking care of a numerical issue.

1.2 Importance

Newton's letter to Collins is viewed as a vital record in the need debate. It shows that Newton had fostered the standards of math by the mid-1670s, years before Leibniz's work.

This letter filled in as the establishment for Newton's cases that Leibniz had counterfeited his thoughts and techniques.

Leibniz's Correspondence with Henry Oldenburg (1676-1677)

Gottfried Wilhelm Leibniz started comparing with Henry Oldenburg, Secretary of the Regal Society, in the last part of the 1670s. These letters assumed a vital part in molding the debate.

2.1 Substance of the Letters

Leibniz traded letters with Oldenburg, examining numerical thoughts and improvements without uncovering the particulars of his documentation or approach.

While Leibniz didn't expressly share his math documentation, he made references to his work on the analytics of infinitesimals.

2.2 Importance

Leibniz's correspondence with Oldenburg showed that he was effectively taken part in conversations with English mathematicians, which would later be refered to as proof of his admittance to Newton's thoughts.

Be that as it may, these letters didn't give decisive proof of counterfeiting or need encroachment.

Leibniz's Distribution of "Nova Methodus master Maximis et Minimis" (1684)

In 1684, Leibniz distributed an original work that presented his documentation and standards of math to the numerical local area.

3.1 Substance of the Distribution

Leibniz's "Nova Methodus ace Maximis et Minimis" (Another Technique for Maxima and Minima) introduced his documentation for analytics, including images like 'd' for separation and '∫' for joining.

The distribution made sense of the standards of separation and mix utilizing his documentation and accentuated the idea of infinitesimals.

3.2 Importance

Leibniz's distribution was a huge achievement in the improvement of math. It exhibited his imaginative documentation, which is still generally utilized in present day math.

The distribution laid out Leibniz as an autonomous designer of math, as he had fostered his documentation and standards without information on Newton's work.

Newton's "De Quadratura Curvarum" (1704)

Newton's work "De Quadratura Curvarum" (On the Quadrature of Bends), distributed in 1704, assumed an essential part in the need question.

4.1 Substance of the Work

In "De Quadratura Curvarum," Newton introduced a portion of his numerical thoughts, including those connected with math and the strategy for fluxions.

He talked about different numerical issues and gave arrangements utilizing his strategy for fluxions.

4.2 Importance

Newton's distribution in 1704, regardless of its moderately late appearance, was an endeavor to affirm his need in the improvement of math.

The work highlighted the way that he had been chipping away at analytics and related numerical issues well before Leibniz's distribution.

The "Commercium Epistolicum" (1712)

The "Commercium Epistolicum" (The Correspondence of Letters), distributed in 1712, is an assortment of letters traded between mathematicians that further energized the need debate.

5.1 Substance of the Aggregation

The "Commercium Epistolicum" included letters traded between Newton, Leibniz, John Collins, and different mathematicians.

The aggregation expected to introduce proof and contentions for the two sides of the debate, with Newton's allegations of copyright infringement and Leibniz's protection of free creation.

5.2 Importance

The distribution of the "Commercium Epistolicum" carried the question into the public eye, igniting broad conversations and discussions inside the numerical local area.

While it didn't determine the question absolutely, it reported the contentions and counterarguments made by both Newton and Leibniz.

Leibniz's "Supplement to the Commercium Epistolicum" (1712)

Because of Newton's allegations in the "Commercium Epistolicum," Leibniz distributed an enhancement to the gathering.

6.1 Substance of the Enhancement

Leibniz's "Supplement to the Commercium Epistolicum" filled in as his safeguard against Newton's allegations.

He repeated his case of autonomous creation, made sense of his documentation and standards, and contended that his math was particular from Newton's strategy for fluxions.

6.2 Importance

Leibniz's enhancement gave further understanding into his point of view on the debate and his endeavors to justify himself against charges of counterfeiting.

It added to the continuous discussion over the need of math.

The Tradition of Correspondence and Distributions

The correspondence and distributions of Newton and Leibniz during the need question left an enduring effect on the historical backdrop of science.

7.1 Acknowledgment of The two Mathematicians

The debate didn't lessen the commitments of one or the other Newton or Leibniz yet rather underlined the significant and persevering through effect of their work on analytics.

Antiquarians of arithmetic perceive both as free fellow benefactors of math.

7.2 Effect on Attribution and Joint effort

The need debate fills in as a useful example, featuring the significance of clear correspondence, legitimate attribution, and coordinated effort among researchers throughout the entire existence of science and math.

7.3 Getting through Effect of Documentations

The documentations and approaches created by both Newton and Leibniz keep on forming the review and practice of math in the advanced time.

Leibniz's documentation, portrayed by images like 'd' for separation and '∫' for reconciliation, stays a principal part of present day math.

4.3 The role of the Royal Society and other mathematicians in the dispute.

The Newton-Leibniz need question, a petulant and getting through episode throughout the entire existence of science, not just elaborate the two chief figures, Sir Isaac Newton and Gottfried Wilhelm Leibniz, yet in addition attracted different mathematicians and establishments. One of the key members in this debate was the Illustrious Society of London, a persuasive logical association of the time. Furthermore, a few mathematicians and researchers ended up caught in the question, either by decision or situation. This paper investigates the urgent pretended by the Regal Society and different mathematicians in escalating and exploring the need question.

The Regal Society's Job

The Regal Society of London assumed a critical part in intervening the question among Newton and Leibniz, as it had individuals who were steady of the two sides.

1.1 The Examination

The Regal Society sent off an authority examination to decide the need of math and to evaluate the allegations made by Newton against Leibniz.

The examination included surveying archives, letters, and declarations from mathematicians who had related with both Newton and Leibniz.

1.2 Blended Gathering

The examination didn't give an unmistakable decision for one or the other Newton or Leibniz.

A few individuals from the Regal Society, especially the people who were steady of Newton, inclined toward his case and saw Leibniz as a copyright infringer.

Others inside the Illustrious Society were more thoughtful to Leibniz and had confidence in his freedom in creating math.

1.3 The Test of Lack of bias

The Illustrious Society confronted the test of keeping up with impartiality in the question, considering that it included individuals with solid devotions to both Newton and Leibniz.

This inside division inside the Imperial Society added to the intricacy of the debate and the trouble in arriving at a convincing choice.

Mathematicians and Researchers Included

A few mathematicians and researchers, some readily and others coincidentally, became engaged with the question by righteousness of their connections with Newton, Leibniz, or both.

2.1 John Collins

John Collins, a mathematician and companion of Newton, assumed a focal part in the debate. He accepted Newton's 1677 letter illustrating his math standards.

Collins additionally compared with Leibniz and imparted numerical plans to him, which later filled Newton's allegations of counterfeiting.

2.2 John Wallis

John Wallis, a conspicuous English mathematician and individual from the Illustrious Society, compared with Leibniz and assumed a part in conversations connected with analytics.

Wallis had a great perspective on Leibniz's work, which impacted the impression of Leibniz inside the Illustrious Society.

2.3 Henry Oldenburg

Henry Oldenburg, the Secretary of the Imperial Society, was a go-between in Leibniz's correspondence with English mathematicians.

Oldenburg was a critical figure in working with conversations among Leibniz and different individuals from the Illustrious Society, despite the fact that he didn't completely grasp the subtleties of math.

2.4 Johann Bernoulli

Johann Bernoulli, a Swiss mathematician, became entangled in the debate when he related with both Newton and Leibniz on different numerical issues.

His letters with Leibniz contained conversations about math and the need question.

Letters and Correspondence

Letters and correspondence assumed a basic part in the improvement of the question, as they filled in as an essential method for correspondence among the mathematicians in question.

3.1 Newton's Letters

Newton's letters, especially his 1677 letter to John Collins, filled in as critical proof for his case of need in the development of analytics.

He utilized his correspondence to exhibit that he had fostered the standards of math some time before Leibniz's work.

3.2 Leibniz's Letters

Leibniz's letters, incorporating his trades with English mathematicians like John Wallis and Henry Oldenburg, were fundamental in laying out the course of events of his associations with individuals from the Illustrious Society.

Leibniz protected his freedom and introduced his own variant of the historical backdrop of analytics in his correspondence.

3.3 Correspondence with Witnesses

Both Newton and Leibniz related with mathematicians who might actually act as observers to help their cases.

These observers, while giving important experiences, frequently had their own

predispositions and translations of occasions.

Influence on the Question

The contribution of the Illustrious Society and different mathematicians significantly affected the course and result of the Newton-Leibniz need debate.

4.1 Absence of an Unmistakable Goal

The question finished without a reasonable goal, with no conclusive decision for one or the other Newton or Leibniz.

The partitioned suppositions inside the Regal Society and the understandings of the proof added to the absence of conclusion.

4.2 Persevering through Strains

The association of different mathematicians and the partitioned loyalties inside the Illustrious Society added to getting through strains in the numerical local area.

The question left a tradition of doubt and contention that persevered for quite a long time.

4.3 Acknowledgment of Autonomous Commitments

In spite of the discussion, both Newton and Leibniz are presently perceived as autonomous prime supporters of math.

Students of history of arithmetic recognize the peculiarity of their commitments and the concurrent advancement of math in Britain and mainland Europe.

Chapter 5

Chapter 5

Chapter 5

The Royal Society's Verdict

The Newton-Leibniz need debate, a warmed contention throughout the entire existence of science, rotated around the subject of who merited recognition for the creation of math. This longstanding fight between Sir Isaac Newton and Gottfried Wilhelm Leibniz reached a crucial stage with the contribution of the Illustrious Society, a persuasive logical association of now is the right time. While trying to resolve the question and decide the legitimate inquirer to the creation of math, the Illustrious Society led an examination and gave a decision. This paper digs into the occasions paving the way to the Illustrious Society's decision, the contentions made by the two sides, and the effect of the choice on the tradition of Newton and Leibniz.

Foundation: The Newton-Leibniz Need Question

Prior to digging into the Illustrious Society's decision, it is fundamental to comprehend the unique situation and course of events of the need question among Newton and Leibniz.

1.1 The Starting points of Math

Both Newton and Leibniz autonomously fostered the standards of math in the late seventeenth hundred years.

Newton's methodology, known as the "strategy for fluxions," depended on paces of progress, while Leibniz's methodology used the documentation of infinitesimals.

1.2 Early Correspondence and Allegations

The question started with a progression of letters traded between mathematicians, including Newton, Leibniz, and their journalists.

Newton blamed Leibniz for copyright infringement, asserting that Leibniz had duplicated his thoughts and techniques.

1.3 The Job of the Imperial Society

The Regal Society, as a noticeable logical establishment, became engaged with the debate because of its individuals' advantages and devotions.

The General public started an examination to decide the need of math and to evaluate the allegations made by Newton against Leibniz.

Newton's Case

Isaac Newton, a noticeable English mathematician and physicist, introduced a convincing case to the Illustrious Society on the side of his need guarantee.

2.1 Newton's Initial Work

Newton attested that he had fostered the standards of analytics, explicitly the "strategy for fluxions," by the mid-1670s.

He refered to his 1677 letter to John Collins, where he had framed the center ideas of his math, as proof of his initial work.

2.2 Allegations of Literary theft

Newton blamed Leibniz for literary theft, fighting that Leibniz had taken his thoughts and strategies.

He highlighted apparent likenesses between his work and Leibniz's documentations and standards as proof of counterfeiting.

2.3 Correspondence and Declarations

Newton gave a course of events of his correspondence different people and mathematicians, stressing his initial work on analytics.

He called upon witnesses who had related with him to confirm his case of need.

Leibniz's Guard

Gottfried Wilhelm Leibniz, a German mathematician and scholar, energetically protected himself against Newton's allegations and communicated his viewpoint to the Illustrious Society.

3.1 Leibniz's Free Innovation

Leibniz fervently prevented Newton's charges from getting copyright infringement, attesting that he had created analytics freely and without admittance to Newton's work.

He contended that his documentation and standards were particular from Newton's.

3.2 Distribution of "Nova Methodus expert Maximis et Minimis" (1684)

Leibniz's distribution of "Nova Methodus star Maximis et Minimis" in 1684 introduced his documentation for analytics, which included images like 'd' for separation and '∫' for combination.

The distribution displayed his imaginative methodology and documentation, underlining his autonomous development.

3.3 The "Supplement to the Commercium Epistolicum" (1712)

Because of Newton's allegations in the "Commercium Epistolicum," Leibniz distributed an enhancement safeguarding his case.

He emphasized his freedom, introduced his form of the historical backdrop of analytics, and contended that his math was unmistakable from Newton's technique for fluxions.

The Illustrious Society's Examination

The Illustrious Society started an examination to assess the cases and counterclaims made by both Newton and Leibniz.

4.1 Assortment of Proof

The examination included surveying a huge range of records, including letters traded among mathematicians and different declarations.

The General public assembled data from the two sides to evaluate the legitimacy of the cases.

4.2 Separated Sentiments

The Regal Society's examination didn't give an unmistakable decision for one or the other Newton or Leibniz.

A few individuals from the General public were strong of Newton and trusted his cases, while others were thoughtful to Leibniz's instance of free development.

4.3 The "Commercium Epistolicum" (1712)

The distribution of the "Commercium Epistolicum" in 1712, a gathering of letters and contentions from the two sides, turned into a focal point of the examination.

The General public surveyed the substance and contentions introduced in this gathering as a feature of its consultations.

The Illustrious Society's Decision

After broad consultations, the Illustrious Society gave a decision in regards to the need question among Newton and Leibniz.

5.1 The Decision's Equivocalness

The Imperial Society's decision was eventually uncertain and didn't absolutely incline toward one or the other Newton or Leibniz.

While the General public recognized the significance of the two mathematicians' commitments, it didn't give a reasonable goal to the debate.

5.2 Acknowledgment of Free Creation

The decision perceived that both Newton and Leibniz had freely made critical commitments to the advancement of analytics.

This affirmation featured the peculiarity of their methodologies and documentations.

5.3 Effect on the Heritage

The Illustrious Society's decision lastingly affected the tradition of both Newton and Leibniz.

While the debate had stressed their relationship and caused harshness, their acknowledgment as free prime supporters of math was saved.

Heritage and Authentic Appraisal

The Newton-Leibniz need question, regardless of the Imperial Society's decision, keeps on being a subject of verifiable interest and discussion in the field of math.

6.1 Acknowledgment as Prime supporters

Today, both Isaac Newton and Gottfried Wilhelm Leibniz are perceived as prime supporters of math.

History specialists of arithmetic recognize their unmistakable commitments, one of a kind methodologies, and the synchronous improvement of math in various regions of the planet.

6.2 Getting through Effect of Documentations

The documentations and approaches created by both Newton and Leibniz keep on molding the review and practice of math in the cutting edge time.

Leibniz's documentation, portrayed by images like 'd' for separation and '∫' for joining, stays a principal part of present day math.

6.3 The Job of the Regal Society

The Regal Society's contribution in the debate fills in as a verifiable illustration of the difficulties looked by foundations in interceding logical discussions.

It highlights the intricacies of deciding need and resolving debates throughout the entire existence of science and math.

5.1 Examination of the Royal Society's investigation into the priority dispute.

The Newton-Leibniz need debate, a hostile episode throughout the entire existence of science, finished in the contribution of the Imperial Society, a conspicuous logical organization of now is the right time. As both Sir Isaac Newton and Gottfried Wilhelm Leibniz made a case for the development of math, the Illustrious Society embraced an examination to decide the need and evaluate the allegations. This paper analyzes the Illustrious Society's examination, diving into its methods, discoveries, and the more extensive ramifications of its job in the debate.

Foundation: The Illustrious Society's Contribution

Prior to analyzing the Illustrious Society's examination, it is essential to comprehend the unique situation and inspiration driving its association in the Newton-Leibniz need question.

1.1 The Logical Environment

The late seventeenth century was a time of extreme logical movement and disclosure.

The Illustrious Society, established in 1660, was a main foundation in advancing and progressing logical exploration.

1.2 The Cases of Newton and Leibniz

Newton and Leibniz had autonomously created analytics, however their methodologies and documentations contrasted fundamentally.

Both made a case for the innovation of math, which made a harsh question between the two mathematicians.

1.3 The Requirement for Goal

Mainstream researchers, including individuals from the Regal Society, perceived the requirement for a goal to the question to guarantee legitimate attribution and credit for the improvement of math.

The Illustrious Society considered itself to be a characteristic discussion for tending to such debates.

The Regal Society's Examination Cycle

The Regal Society started a proper examination concerning the need question among Newton and Leibniz. This segment looks at the vital parts of the examination interaction.

2.1 Assortment of Proof

The examination included the assortment of a significant volume of proof, including letters, distributions, and declarations from people who had compared with both Newton and Leibniz.

The point was to survey the course of events of their separate commitments and cooperations with different mathematicians.

2.2 Thoughts and Advisory groups

The Regal Society laid out advisory groups and boards to audit the proof and lead consultations.

These panels were made out of individuals from the General public, some of whom had individual or scholarly connections to one or the other Newton or Leibniz.

2.3 The "Commercium Epistolicum" (1712)

The distribution of the "Commercium Epistolicum," a gathering of letters and contentions from the two sides, turned into a focal point of the examination.

The General public explored the substance and contentions introduced in this arrangement as a component of its considerations.

2.4 Interior Divisions

The Regal Society confronted inner divisions among its individuals, with some supporting Newton and others thoughtful to Leibniz's cases.

These divisions confounded the examination and added to its equivocal result.

Uncertainty in the Decision

The Regal Society's decision, gave after its examination, was set apart by equivocalness and didn't offer a reasonable goal to the question.

3.1 Acknowledgment of Free Creation

The decision recognized that both Newton and Leibniz had autonomously made huge commitments to the improvement of analytics.

It perceived their unmistakable methodologies and documentations.

3.2 Absence of Convincing Proof

The General public's decision didn't absolutely incline toward one or the other Newton or Leibniz.

The examination neglected to deliver convincing proof that would definitively lay out one mathematician's need over the other.

3.3 Ramifications of Uncertainty

The uncertain decision had suggestions for the tradition of both Newton and Leibniz, as it left space for continuous discussion and conflict.

It likewise featured the difficulties of settling questions throughout the entire existence of science and math.

The Decision's Effect

The Illustrious Society's decision lastingly affected the tradition of both Newton and Leibniz and on the more extensive history of science.

4.1 Acknowledgment as Prime supporters

Today, both Newton and Leibniz are perceived as fellow benefactors of math.

History specialists of arithmetic recognize their free commitments, unmistakable methodologies, and the concurrent improvement of math.

4.2 Getting through Tradition of Documentations

The documentations and approaches created by both Newton and Leibniz keep on molding the review and practice of math in the cutting edge period.

Leibniz's documentation, portrayed by images like 'd' for separation and '∫' for reconciliation, stays indispensable to present day analytics.

4.3 Authentic Appraisal

The Regal Society's contribution in the debate fills in as a verifiable illustration of the difficulties looked by organizations in intervening logical discussions.

It highlights the intricacies of deciding need and resolving debates throughout the entire existence of science and math.

Illustrations Learned

The Newton-Leibniz need question, as inspected from the perspective of the Illustrious Society's examination, offers significant illustrations and bits of knowledge.

5.1 The Significance of Legitimate Attribution

The question features the meaning of appropriate attribution and credit in logical undertakings.

It fills in as a sign of the requirement for clear documentation and correspondence of

logical commitments.

5.2 Equivocalness in Verifiable Decisions

Authentic examinations and decisions, like that of the Imperial Society, may not necessarily in all cases give clear goals to complex questions.

Uncertainty can leave space for progressing understanding and discussion, highlighting the liquid idea of verifiable appraisals.

5.3 Coordinated effort and Participation

The debate accentuates the significance of coordinated effort and collaboration among researchers and mathematicians.

It fills in as a wake up call about the possible results of contention and conflict in established researchers.

5.2 The findings and conclusions of the Royal Society's report.

The Newton-Leibniz need debate, a quarrelsome episode throughout the entire existence of math, finished in an examination by the Regal Society, an esteemed logical foundation of the time. The essential objective of this examination was to decide the legitimate inquirer to the creation of analytics between Sir Isaac Newton and Gottfried Wilhelm Leibniz. This paper digs into the discoveries and finishes of the Illustrious Society's report, investigating the critical components of the examination, the proof introduced, and a definitive decision that lastingly affects the tradition of the two mathematicians.

The Analytical Interaction

Prior to diving into the discoveries and ends, it is fundamental to comprehend the analytical interaction embraced by the Imperial Society.

1.1 Assortment of Proof

The examination included a fastidious assortment of proof, including letters, distributions, and declarations from people who had related with both Newton and Leibniz.

The goal was to lay out a timetable of their separate commitments to math and cooperations with different mathematicians.

1.2 Councils and Considerations

The Imperial Society laid out boards of trustees and boards made out of its individuals to audit the proof and lead considerations.

These advisory groups were depended with the assignment of assessing the cases and counterclaims made by both Newton and Leibniz.

1.3 The Job of the "Commercium Epistolicum"

The distribution of the "Commercium Epistolicum" in 1712, a gathering of letters and contentions from the two sides, turned into a focal point of the examination.

The General public explored the substance and contentions introduced in this gathering as a component of its thoughts.

1.4 Inner Divisions

The Regal Society confronted inner divisions among its individuals, with some supporting Newton and others thoughtful to Leibniz's cases.

These divisions muddled the examination and added to its uncertain result.

Key Discoveries of the Examination

The Illustrious Society's examination yielded a few key discoveries that shed light on the need debate among Newton and Leibniz.

2.1 Affirmation of Autonomous Commitments

The examination recognized that both Isaac Newton and Gottfried Wilhelm Leibniz had autonomously made significant commitments to the advancement of math.

It perceived their particular methodologies and documentations.

2.2 Acknowledgment of Newton's Initial Work

The examination confirmed that Newton had fostered the standards of math, especially his "strategy for fluxions," by the mid-1670s.

Newton's 1677 letter to John Collins, framing his math standards, was considered critical proof of his initial work.

2.3 Leibniz's Free Innovation

The examination perceived Leibniz's fiery safeguard of his free development of math.

It highlighted that Leibniz had fostered his documentation and standards without admittance to Newton's work.

2.4 Uncertainty in the Decision

Maybe the most basic finding was the uncertainty in the decision, which didn't conclusively lean toward one or the other Newton or Leibniz.

The examination neglected to deliver convincing proof that would definitively lay out one mathematician's need over the other.

Ends and Suggestions

The Regal Society's report prompted a few huge ends and suggestions that keep on molding the tradition of Newton and Leibniz and our comprehension of the historical backdrop of science.

3.1 Acknowledgment as Prime supporters

Today, both Newton and Leibniz are perceived as prime supporters of analytics.

Students of history of math recognize their free commitments and their exceptional ways to deal with analytics.

3.2 Tradition of Documentations

The documentations and approaches created by both Newton and Leibniz keep on being essential to the review and practice of math.

Leibniz's documentation, portrayed by images like 'd' for separation and '∫' for joining, stays indispensable to present day analytics.

3.3 The Uncertainty of Verifiable Decisions

The Regal Society's report fills in to act as an illustration of the difficulties intrinsic in settling complex verifiable questions.

It features the uncertainty that can encompass authentic decisions, leaving space for continuous translation and discussion.

3.4 Illustrations Learned

The question and the Illustrious Society's examination underline the significance of appropriate attribution and credit in logical undertakings.

They likewise highlight the meaning of joint effort and collaboration among researchers and mathematicians.

Verifiable Evaluation

The discoveries and finishes of the Illustrious Society's report have formed the authentic appraisal of the Newton-Leibniz need question.

4.1 A Verifiable Achievement

The examination is seen as a verifiable achievement throughout the entire existence of math, as it endeavored to address a huge question in an efficient and coordinated way.

It fills in as a source of perspective point for figuring out the commitments of Newton and Leibniz to math.

4.2 Tradition of The two Mathematicians

Both Newton and Leibniz are praised for their commitments to arithmetic, with their names firmly connected with the improvement of analytics.

Their autonomous work and one of a kind documentations have left a getting through inheritance.

4.3 Proceeded with Discussion and Grant

The equivocalness of the Illustrious Society's decision has energized continuous discussion and grant in regards to the question.

Mathematicians, history specialists, and researchers keep on inspecting the proof and reconsider the commitments of Newton and Leibniz.

5.3 The impact of the Royal Society's decision on the reputations of Newton and Leibniz.

The Newton-Leibniz need debate, a harsh contention throughout the entire existence of science, made a permanent imprint on the traditions of Sir Isaac Newton and Gottfried Wilhelm Leibniz. The Imperial Society, a noticeable logical establishment of the time, assumed a vital part in endeavoring to resolve the question through its examination. This paper investigates the effect of the Imperial Society's choice on the notorieties of Newton and Leibniz, analyzing how their commitments to math were seen in the consequence of the examination and how their heritages have advanced over the long haul.

The Setting of the Need Question

Prior to evaluating the effect of the Regal Society's choice, it is essential to comprehend the setting of the need debate among Newton and Leibniz.

1.1 Free Improvement of Math

Both Newton and Leibniz freely fostered the standards of analytics in the late seventeenth hundred years.

Newton's "strategy for fluxions" and Leibniz's documentation based approach addressed particular ways to a similar numerical objective.

1.2 Allegations of Copyright infringement

The question started with allegations of counterfeiting, with Newton asserting that Leibniz had duplicated his thoughts and techniques.

Correspondence and distributions became fundamental to the question, with the two sides putting forth their viewpoint through letters and expositions.

1.3 The Job of the Regal Society

The Regal Society, as a regarded logical foundation, became engaged with the question because of its individuals' advantages and loyalties.

The General public directed an examination to decide the need of math and survey the legitimacy of Newton's allegations against Leibniz.

Influence on Newton's Standing

The Imperial Society's choice significantly affected the standing of Sir Isaac Newton.

2.1 Acknowledgment of Early Work

The Imperial Society's choice attested Newton's case to having fostered the standards of analytics early, especially through his 1677 letter to John Collins.

It perceived the meaning of his "strategy for fluxions" as a spearheading commitment to the field.

2.2 Uncertain Decision

While the Regal Society recognized Newton's initial work, the decision was at last vague and didn't offer a reasonable justification.

The Newton-Leibniz need debate, a harsh contention throughout the entire existence of science, made a permanent imprint on the traditions of Sir Isaac Newton and Gottfried Wilhelm Leibniz. The Imperial Society, a noticeable logical establishment of the time, assumed a vital part in endeavoring to resolve the question through its examination. This paper investigates the effect of the Imperial Society's choice on the notorieties of Newton and Leibniz, analyzing how their commitments to math were seen in the consequence of the examination and how their heritages have advanced over the long haul.

The Setting of the Need Question

Prior to evaluating the effect of the Regal Society's choice, it is essential to comprehend the setting of the need debate among Newton and Leibniz.

1.1 Free Improvement of Math

Both Newton and Leibniz freely fostered the standards of analytics in the late seventeenth hundred years.

Newton's "strategy for fluxions" and Leibniz's documentation based approach addressed particular ways to a similar numerical objective.

1.2 Allegations of Copyright infringement

The question started with allegations of counterfeiting, with Newton asserting that Leibniz had duplicated his thoughts and techniques.

Correspondence and distributions became fundamental to the question, with the two sides putting forth their viewpoint through letters and expositions.

1.3 The Job of the Regal Society

The Regal Society, as a regarded logical foundation, became engaged with the question because of its individuals' advantages and loyalties.

The General public directed an examination to decide the need of math and survey the legitimacy of Newton's allegations against Leibniz.

Influence on Newton's Standing

The Imperial Society's choice significantly affected the standing of Sir Isaac Newton.

2.1 Acknowledgment of Early Work

The Imperial Society's choice attested Newton's case to having fostered the standards of analytics early, especially through his 1677 letter to John Collins.

It perceived the meaning of his "strategy for fluxions" as a spearheading commitment to the field.

2.2 Uncertain Decision

While the Regal Society recognized Newton's initial work, the decision was at last vague and didn't offer a reasonable justification.

The absence of a definitive decision left space for waiting questions about the degree of Leibniz's reliance on Newton's thoughts.

2.3 Inheritance as a Mathematician

In spite of the vagueness of the decision, Newton's heritage as a mathematician stayed significant.

His commitments to analytics, as well as his more extensive work in math and material science, kept on being praised.

2.4 Pressures and Disdain

The question had stressed Newton's relationship with individual mathematicians and researchers.

The unpleasant allegations and public quarrel had prompted hatred inside mainstream researchers.

Influence on Leibniz's Standing

The Regal Society's choice likewise lastingly affected the standing of Gottfried Wilhelm Leibniz.

3.1 Acknowledgment of Autonomous Creation

The Regal Society's decision perceived Leibniz's guard of his free innovation of analytics.

It highlighted that Leibniz had fostered his documentation and standards without admittance to Newton's work.

3.2 The Questionable Decision

Like Newton, Leibniz didn't get an unmistakable justification from the Illustrious Society's decision.

While it perceived his free development, it didn't completely exonerate him of allegations of counterfeiting.

3.3 Heritage as a Mathematician

Leibniz's heritage as a mathematician and logician stayed in salvageable shape.

His documentation based way to deal with analytics, which presented images like 'd' for separation and '∫' for combination, made a critical imprint on math.

3.4 Philosophical Commitments

Leibniz's standing reached out past math. His commitments to reasoning, rationale, and transcendentalism kept on being exceptionally respected.

Advancing Discernments Over the long run

The effect of the Imperial Society's choice on the notorieties of Newton and Leibniz

advanced over the long run.

4.1 Acknowledgment of Prime supporters

Present day authentic appraisals perceive both Newton and Leibniz as prime supporters of math.

The decision's affirmation of their free commitments has turned into the overall view.

4.2 Getting through Tradition of Documentations

Leibniz's documentation based approach stays an essential piece of present day math.

His images for separation and joining are as yet utilized today.

4.3 Proceeded with Discussion and Grant

The question, and the Regal Society's part in it, has filled continuous discussion and grant.

Mathematicians, antiquarians, and researchers keep on investigating the subtleties of the question and reconsider the commitments of the two mathematicians.The absence of a definitive decision left space for waiting questions about the degree of Leibniz's reliance on Newton's thoughts.

2.3 Inheritance as a Mathematician

In spite of the vagueness of the decision, Newton's heritage as a mathematician stayed significant.

His commitments to analytics, as well as his more extensive work in math and material science, kept on being praised.

2.4 Pressures and Disdain

The question had stressed Newton's relationship with individual mathematicians and researchers.

The unpleasant allegations and public quarrel had prompted hatred inside mainstream researchers.

Influence on Leibniz's Standing

The Regal Society's choice likewise lastingly affected the standing of Gottfried Wilhelm Leibniz.

3.1 Acknowledgment of Autonomous Creation

The Regal Society's decision perceived Leibniz's guard of his free innovation of analytics.

It highlighted that Leibniz had fostered his documentation and standards without admittance to Newton's work.

3.2 The Questionable Decision

Like Newton, Leibniz didn't get an unmistakable justification from the Illustrious Society's decision.

While it perceived his free development, it didn't completely exonerate him of allegations of counterfeiting.

3.3 Heritage as a Mathematician

Leibniz's heritage as a mathematician and logician stayed in salvageable shape.

His documentation based way to deal with analytics, which presented images like 'd' for separation and '∫' for combination, made a critical imprint on math.

3.4 Philosophical Commitments

Leibniz's standing reached out past math. His commitments to reasoning, rationale, and transcendentalism kept on being exceptionally respected.

Advancing Discernments Over the long run

The effect of the Imperial Society's choice on the notorieties of Newton and Leibniz advanced over the long run.

4.1 Acknowledgment of Prime supporters

Present day authentic appraisals perceive both Newton and Leibniz as prime supporters of math.

The decision's affirmation of their free commitments has turned into the overall view.

4.2 Getting through Tradition of Documentations

Leibniz's documentation based approach stays an essential piece of present day math.

His images for separation and joining are as yet utilized today.

4.3 Proceeded with Discussion and Grant

The question, and the Regal Society's part in it, has filled continuous discussion and grant.

Mathematicians, antiquarians, and researchers keep on investigating the subtleties of the question and reconsider the commitments of the two mathematicians.

Chapter 6

Chapter 6

International Controversy and Legacy

The Newton-Leibniz need question, a profoundly combative and persevering through contention throughout the entire existence of math, rose above public lines and turned into a global peculiarity. This question, which spun around the creation of analytics, involved two of the main mathematicians of the seventeenth 100 years, Sir Isaac Newton and Gottfried Wilhelm Leibniz. It not just formed the traditions of these two mathematicians yet additionally left a significant effect on the improvement of math, the way of thinking of science, and how debates in established researchers are made due. This article investigates the global debate encompassing the Newton-Leibniz need question and digs into the enduring heritage it has left on the universe of arithmetic and then some.

The Internationalization of the Question

1.1 Development of the Debate

The question among Newton and Leibniz at first started as a confidential fight among English and German mathematicians yet immediately heightened to a global discussion.

The trading of letters and distributions between mathematicians from various nations assumed a vital part in the debate's internationalization.

1.2 Mainland Europe versus Britain

The debate took on a nationalistic tone, with mathematicians in Britain, where Newton was based, supporting his case, while those in mainland Europe, where Leibniz lived, mobilized behind him.

This division escalated the debate and added to its global person.

1.3 More extensive European Interest

Mathematicians from different European nations, including France, the Netherlands, and Switzerland, effectively took part in the debate.

They took part in the trading of letters, articles, and distributions, further filling the discussion.

The Job of Worldwide Correspondence

Worldwide correspondence was a urgent part of the Newton-Leibniz need debate, as it worked with the trading of thoughts, allegations, and contentions among mathematicians from various nations.

2.1 Letters and Distributions

Mathematicians on the two sides of the question traded various letters and distributed papers and compositions to put forth their viewoints.

These letters and distributions assumed a focal part in scattering the debate's subtleties and contentions to a more extensive worldwide crowd.

2.2 Leibniz's Correspondence

Gottfried Wilhelm Leibniz kept a broad organization of reporters across Europe.

He utilized his letters to safeguard his autonomous development of analytics and to earn support for his objective.

2.3 French Inclusion

French mathematicians, including Pierre Varignon and Nicolas Malebranche, became engaged with the question, especially in protecting Leibniz's work.

French mathematicians assumed a huge part in the internationalization of the debate.

2.4 Swiss Mathematicians

Swiss mathematicians, like Johann Bernoulli and his sibling Jakob Bernoulli, compared with both Newton and Leibniz.

Their letters contained conversations about math and the need debate, further featuring the worldwide element of the contention.

The Illustrious Society and Worldwide Relations

The contribution of the Regal Society of London, an esteemed logical organization, added a global aspect to the debate.

3.1 The Illustrious Society's Examination

The Illustrious Society's choice to examine the debate raised it to a worldwide stage.

The examination included inspecting proof and declarations from mathematicians across Europe.

3.2 Mainland Discernments

The examination was seen distinctively on the landmass and in Britain.

In mainland Europe, the Illustrious Society was seen with doubt, with allegations of predisposition for Newton.

3.3 Effect on Worldwide Relations

The debate stressed global relations inside established researchers.

It featured the intricacies of overseeing debates including unmistakable researchers from various nations.

Tradition of the Debate

The Newton-Leibniz need debate left a significant and getting through heritage in a few key regions.

4.1 Effect on Science

The question added to the advancement of analytics and the refinement of numerical documentation.

Leibniz's emblematic documentation, which assumed a huge part in the debate, stays a foundation of current science.

4.2 The Way of thinking of Science

The debate brought up significant issues about need and credit in science and math.

It prompted conversations about the idea of licensed innovation and the morals of logical disclosure.

4.3 Effect on Verifiable Technique

The debate underscored the significance of thorough authentic philosophy in surveying the commitments of researchers.

History specialists of science have since grown more nuanced ways to deal with grasping logical debates.

4.4 Molding Present day Perspectives

The debate helped shape present day sees on the historical backdrop of math and the acknowledgment of various supporters of logical leap forwards.

Newton and Leibniz are currently perceived as prime supporters of analytics.

6.1 The spread of the calculus controversy beyond England and Germany.

The analytics discussion between Sir Isaac Newton and Gottfried Wilhelm Leibniz was not restricted to Britain and Germany. It immediately spread past these two countries and formed into a global question that elaborate mathematicians and researchers from different nations in Europe. This article investigates the engendering of the analytics

contention, looking at how it rose above public limits and involved mathematicians from France, Switzerland, the Netherlands, and other European districts. It likewise dives into the vital commitments and points of view of these global entertainers in the question.

The Beginnings of the Debate

1.1 Newton's Initial Work in Britain

Sir Isaac Newton, an English mathematician and physicist, fostered his analytics strategies in the late seventeenth 100 years.

His "technique for fluxions" addressed a critical jump in numerical comprehension.

1.2 Leibniz's Free Development in Germany

Gottfried Wilhelm Leibniz, a German mathematician and rationalist, freely fostered his documentation based math during a similar period.

Leibniz's emblematic documentation, including 'd' for separation and '∫' for coordination, recognized his methodology.

1.3 Early Correspondence

The debate at first started with private trades of letters between mathematicians in Britain and Germany.

Allegations of counterfeiting and need claims filled the contention.

Association of France

France assumed a huge part in the internationalization of the math debate.

2.1 Mathematicians' Help for Leibniz

French mathematicians, including Pierre Varignon and Nicolas Malebranche, effectively upheld Leibniz's case of free creation.

They compared with Leibniz and distributed articles protecting his documentation based analytics.

2.2 The Paris Institute of Sciences

The Paris Foundation of Sciences became entangled in the debate, with individuals favoring one side on the side of one or the other Newton or Leibniz.

The Foundation's inclusion raised the debate to a worldwide stage.

2.3 Job of the "Commercium Epistolicum"

The distribution of the "Commercium Epistolicum" in 1712, a gathering of letters and contentions from the two sides, had a critical effect in France.

French mathematicians firmly analyzed its items and added to the continuous discussion.

Swiss Mathematicians and Their Point of view

Swiss mathematicians, especially the Bernoulli siblings, assumed a focal part in the math debate.

3.1 Correspondence with Newton and Leibniz

Johann Bernoulli and his sibling Jakob Bernoulli related with both Newton and Leibniz.

Their letters contained conversations about analytics and the need debate.

3.2 Help for Leibniz

The Bernoulli siblings were at first strong of Leibniz's documentation based analytics.

Their association reinforced Leibniz's situation in the question.

3.3 The Bernoulli Challenge

Johann Bernoulli gave a popular test as a numerical issue in 1696, known as the "Bernoulli Challenge," welcoming mathematicians to settle it utilizing their analytics strategies.

This challenge additionally heightened the debate and pulled in the consideration of mathematicians from different nations.

The Job of the Netherlands

The Netherlands likewise saw critical cooperation in the analytics debate.

4.1 Dutch Mathematicians

Dutch mathematicians, like Willem 's Gravesande and Johann van Waveren Hudde, participated in the debate.

They composed letters and distributed articles examining the contending cases of Newton and Leibniz.

4.2 Hudde's Letter to Leibniz

Johann van Waveren Hudde, a noticeable Dutch mathematician, related with Leibniz.

Hudde's letter to Leibniz communicated help for his documentation based math and added to the developing global discussion.

More extensive European Inclusion

The analytics debate reached out past France, Switzerland, and the Netherlands, drawing the consideration and investment of mathematicians from other European locales.

5.1 Job of Italy

Italian mathematicians, like Tommaso Ceva, communicated interest in the question.

While Italy didn't assume a focal part, it mirrored the more extensive European commitment to the discussion.

5.2 Effect on Future Mathematicians

The analytics contention impacted people in the future of mathematicians who were enlivened by the continuous discussion.

The debate left a heritage that kept on reverberating inside the numerical local area.

6.2 The reactions of mathematicians and scholars across Europe.

The analytics debate, which rotated around the cases of Sir Isaac Newton and Gottfried Wilhelm Leibniz to the innovation of math, drew the consideration and responses of mathematicians and researchers from across Europe. This article investigates the different responses of these people to the contention, revealing insight into the effect of the question on the more extensive European numerical local area and the scholarly talk of the time.

The Spread of the Debate

1.1 Rise of the Debate

The math debate started as a confidential fight between mathematicians in Britain and Germany however immediately heightened.

The trading of letters and distributions expanded the debate's arrive at past public limits.

1.2 France: Protectors of Leibniz

French mathematicians, like Pierre Varignon and Nicolas Malebranche, effectively upheld Leibniz's case of free creation.

Their commitments raised the debate to a global stage.

1.3 Switzerland: The Bernoulli Siblings

Swiss mathematicians Johann and Jakob Bernoulli compared with both Newton and Leibniz and assumed a focal part in the debate.

Their test and backing for Leibniz added profundity to the global talk.

1.4 The Netherlands: Dutch Inclusion

Dutch mathematicians, including Willem 's Gravesande and Johann van Waveren Hudde, took part in the debate.

They composed letters and distributed papers talking about the contending cases of

Newton and Leibniz.

The French Point of view

France arose as a conspicuous community for the guard of Leibniz's documentation based math.

2.1 French Mathematicians

French mathematicians were partitioned in their help for one or the other Newton or Leibniz.Some, as Varignon and Malebranche, effectively guarded Leibniz's documentation and standards.

2.2 The Paris Foundation of Sciences

The Paris Foundation of Sciences became entangled in the question, with individuals favoring one side.

The Institute's contribution added power and exposure to the worldwide discussion.

2.3 The "Commercium Epistolicum"

The distribution of the "Commercium Epistolicum" in 1712 assumed a vital part in France.

French mathematicians firmly analyzed its items and added to the continuous discussion.

The Swiss Point of view

Swiss mathematicians, especially the Bernoulli siblings, connected profoundly with the analytics discussion.

3.1 Correspondence with Newton and Leibniz

Johann and Jakob Bernoulli compared broadly with both Newton and Leibniz.

Their letters contained numerical conversations and appraisals of the need question.

3.2 Help for Leibniz

The Bernoulli siblings at first upheld Leibniz's documentation based analytics.

Their "Bernoulli Challenge" in 1696 welcomed mathematicians to tackle an issue utilizing their analytics techniques, further strengthening the discussion.

3.3 Numerical Commitments

Johann Bernoulli made huge numerical commitments during the question.

His work added to the scholarly talk encompassing math and the cases of Newton and Leibniz.

The Dutch Point of view

Dutch mathematicians effectively took part in the analytics contention, communicating fluctuating levels of help for one or the other side.

4.1 Dutch Mathematicians

Mathematicians in the Netherlands, for example, 's Gravesande and Hudde, added to the discussion.

They composed letters and distributed papers that examined the cases of Newton and Leibniz.

4.2 Hudde's Letter to Leibniz

Johann van Waveren Hudde, a Dutch mathematician, compared with Leibniz and communicated help for his documentation based analytics.

Hudde's letter added to the worldwide conversation.

Effect on Other European Districts

While France, Switzerland, and the Netherlands assumed conspicuous parts, the math discussion likewise resounded in other European locales.

5.1 Italian Interest

Italian mathematicians, including Tommaso Ceva, communicated interest in the debate.

While Italy didn't assume a focal part, it mirrored the more extensive European commitment to the debate.

5.2 Effect on Future Mathematicians

The debate left a getting through influence on people in the future of mathematicians.

The discussion filled in as a wellspring of motivation and added to the improvement of math as a field of study.

6.3The lasting legacy of the dispute on mathematics, notation, and calculus education.

The Newton-Leibniz analytics question, which enthralled the numerical world in the late seventeenth and mid eighteenth hundreds of years, left a getting through heritage that rose above the individual contention between Sir Isaac Newton and Gottfried Wilhelm Leibniz. This exposition investigates the significant and enduring effect of the question on arithmetic, numerical documentation, and math instruction, featuring how it formed the advancement of these fields and keeps on impacting them today.

The Improvement of Math

1.1. Free Innovation Recognized

The analytics debate eventually perceived the free commitments of both Newton and Leibniz to the advancement of math.

This affirmation established the groundwork for the fellow benefactor status they hold throughout the entire existence of math.

1.2. The Idea of Cutoff points

One of the persevering through traditions of math is the idea of cutoff points, which arose out of crafted by both Newton and Leibniz.

The idea of cutoff points became central to math and given a thorough system to figuring out subordinates and integrals.

1.3. Thorough Numerical Approach

The question underscored the requirement for a thorough numerical philosophy to help and legitimize new numerical ideas.

This accentuation on meticulousness turned into a sign of numerical exploration and instruction.

Documentation: The Leibnizian Heritage

2.1. Leibniz's Emblematic Documentation

Maybe the main commitment of Leibniz to science was his improvement of an emblematic documentation for math.

Images like 'd' for separation and '∫' for combination changed the field.

2.2. Omnipresence of Leibnizian Documentation

Leibniz's representative documentation immediately acquired acknowledgment and turned into the norm for math.

It stays a vital piece of current analytics, giving a succinct and strong method for communicating numerical thoughts.

2.3. Development of Numerical Documentation

Leibniz's documentation affected the development of numerical documentation past analytics.

It set a trend for the improvement of proficient and natural documentation frameworks in different parts of science.

Instructional method and Math Training

3.1. The Spread of Analytics Training

The analytics debate prodded interest and conversation about the instructing of math.

It added to the spread of analytics training across Europe and then some.

3.2. Advancement of Math Educational programs

The need to show analytics efficiently prompted the advancement of math educational plans.

Course readings and educational materials were made to work with the instructing and learning of math.

3.3. Influence on Math Instruction

The debate by implication influenced science training by featuring the significance of primary ideas and thorough thinking.

It affected educational methodologies in math, underlining lucidity and accuracy in numerical article.

The Impact on Numerical Culture

4.1. Moral Contemplations

The analytics debate brought moral contemplations up in the act of math.

It incited conversations about the legitimate attribution of thoughts and the morals of logical need.

4.2. Established researchers

The question formed the elements of established researchers, underscoring the worth of cooperation and the significance of keeping up with academic respectability.

4.3. Scholarly Discussions

Scholarly discussions ignited by the question stretched out past the limits of analytics.

They affected more extensive conversations about the way of thinking of science and the idea of logical disclosure.

The Advanced Point of view

5.1. Fellow benefactor Status

Today, both Isaac Newton and Gottfried Wilhelm Leibniz are praised as fellow benefactors of math.

The question's affirmation of their autonomous commitments stays the overall view.

5.2. Leibniz's Documentation

Leibniz's emblematic documentation keeps on being broadly utilized in arithmetic.

It works on complex articulations and cultivates clearness in numerical correspondence.

5.3. Math Schooling

The tradition of the debate is clear in present day math training.

Thorough numerical thinking and clear documentation stay fundamental parts of math educational plans.

5.4. Moral Contemplations

The math question has left an enduring engraving on the morals of attribution and need in logical exploration.

It fills in as a verifiable sign of the moral obligations of researchers and mathematicians.

Chapter 7

Chapter 7

Beyond Calculus:
The Mathematicians' Other Contributions

While Sir Isaac Newton and Gottfried Wilhelm Leibniz are principally known for their commitments to math and the renowned question that followed, the two mathematicians made significant commitments to many fields inside science and then some. This article investigates the less popular features of their work, revealing insight into the different and getting through commitments of Newton and Leibniz in regions like calculation, polynomial math, physical science, and reasoning. It highlights the more extensive effect of their scholarly undertakings past the domain of analytics.

Sir Isaac Newton's Commitments

1.1. The Principia Mathematica

Newton's "Philosophiæ Naturalis Principia Mathematica" (Numerical Standards of Normal Way of thinking), frequently alluded to as the Principia, is a pivotal work.

It presented the laws of movement and widespread attractive energy, reforming the field of physical science.

1.2. Commitments to Calculation

Newton made critical commitments to calculation, remembering his work for the arrangement of cubic bends.

His creative ways to deal with calculation stretched out past the limits of math.

1.3. Polynomial math and Conditions

Newton created procedures for settling polynomial conditions and frameworks of conditions.

His work laid the basis for logarithmic strategies that would become fundamental in science.

1.4. Optics

Newton directed examinations and examinations in optics, prompting the advancement of the hypothesis of varieties.

His work in optics assumed a significant part in how we might interpret light and variety.

1.5. Logical Technique

Newton's way to deal with logical request, described by exact trial and error and numerical meticulousness, turned into a model for the logical technique.

His principled methodology keeps on impacting logical examination.

Gottfried Wilhelm Leibniz's Commitments

2.1. The Leibnizian Analytics

Leibniz's documentation based math has left a getting through heritage.

His representative documentation, including 'd' for separation and '∫' for mix, keeps on being essential in math.

2.2. Monadology

Leibniz's way of thinking of monads, as illustrated in his "Monadology," added to supernatural conversations.

His thoughts on the idea of the real world and substance stay compelling in way of thinking.

2.3. Parallel Framework

Leibniz is credited with the development of the twofold framework, a foundation of current software engineering.

His work established the groundwork for computational progressions.

2.4. Combinatorics

Leibniz made eminent commitments to combinatorics, including the improvement of the binomial hypothesis.

His work in this space has applications in different fields, including measurements and software engineering.

2.5. Legitimate and Strategic Commitments

Leibniz filled in as a negotiator and legitimate master, adding to conversations on worldwide regulation.

His discretionary endeavors pointed toward cultivating joint effort among European countries.

The Effect on Current Arithmetic

3.1. Newton's Impact

Newton's work in analytics and numerical material science remains basic.

His laws of movement and general attractive energy have given the premise to the investigation of mechanics and heavenly mechanics.

3.2. Leibniz's Documentation

Leibniz's representative documentation for analytics is still broadly utilized in math.

It gives a brief and strong method for communicating numerical thoughts.

3.3. Computational Progressions

Leibniz's parallel framework laid the foundation for present day processing.

The paired framework's significance in software engineering couldn't possibly be more significant.

3.4. Philosophical Impact

Both Newton's and Leibniz's philosophical commitments have had an enduring effect.

Their thoughts keep on forming conversations in transcendentalism, epistemology, and the way of thinking of science.

3.5. Moral and Lawful Contemplations

Leibniz's association in lawful and political undertakings highlights the interdisciplinary idea of his commitments.

His thoughts on global collaboration stay pertinent in the cutting edge world.

Contemporary Significance

4.1. Logical Approach

Newton's principled way to deal with science stays a foundation of logical philosophy.

His accentuation on observational examination and numerical meticulousness illuminates contemporary logical exploration.

4.2. Software engineering

Leibniz's double framework fills in as the underpinning of current figuring.

Progresses in computerized innovation owe an obligation to his creative reasoning.

4.3. Numerical Documentation

Leibniz's documentation keeps on working with numerical correspondence and articulation.

It works on complex numerical ideas, helping the two mathematicians and researchers.

4.4. Philosophical Talk

The philosophical thoughts of both Newton and Leibniz keep on motivating contemporary philosophical conversations.

Their commitments to power and epistemology are as yet dependent upon investigation and understanding.

7.1A look at the broader contributions of Newton and Leibniz to mathematics and science.

Sir Isaac Newton and Gottfried Wilhelm Leibniz, two transcending figures throughout the entire existence of science and math, are most popular for their commitments to analytics and the renowned need question that followed. Notwithstanding, their effect stretches out a long ways past the domain of math, enveloping a different cluster of fields in math, physical science, reasoning, and that's only the tip of the iceberg. This exposition gives a top to bottom assessment of the more extensive commitments of Newton and Leibniz to math and science, featuring the significant and enduring impact of their thoughts and developments.

Newton's More extensive Commitments

1.1. The Principia Mathematica

Newton's most eminent work, the "Philosophiæ Naturalis Principia Mathematica" (Numerical Standards of Regular Way of thinking), generally known as the Principia, changed the field of physical science.

In it, he figured out the laws of movement and widespread attraction, giving a bound together system to make sense of divine and earthbound peculiarities.

1.2. Numerical Thoroughness

Newton's accentuation on numerical thoroughness raised the guidelines of logical examination.

His thorough way to deal with logical request established the groundwork for present day physical science and arithmetic.

1.3. Commitments to Optics

Newton's work in optics prompted pivotal revelations, including the deterioration of light into its constituent tones.

His examinations with crystals and the improvement of the hypothesis of varieties extended how we might interpret light and vision.

1.4. The Advancement of Analytics

Newton's autonomous improvement of analytics, known as the "technique for fluxions," altogether added to the progression of science.

His work in math laid out a deliberate way to deal with concentrating on paces of progress and gathering.

1.5. Math and Polynomial math

Newton made significant commitments to math, especially in the grouping of cubic bends.

His advancements in variable based math included procedures for settling polynomial conditions and frameworks of conditions.

Leibniz's More extensive Commitments

2.1. Emblematic Documentation for Analytics

Leibniz's most getting through commitment to science was his emblematic documentation for math.

His documentation, including 'd' for separation and '∫' for combination, stays basic in current math.

2.2. Monadology and Mysticism

Leibniz's philosophical work, "Monadology," presented the idea of monads, which added to conversations in mysticism.

His thoughts on the idea of the real world, substance, and pre-laid out amicability affected resulting philosophical idea.

2.3. Creation of the Paired Framework

Leibniz is credited with creating the paired numeral framework, a key idea in software engineering.

His work laid the foundation for computational headways and computerized innovation.

2.4. Combinatorics and the Binomial Hypothesis

Leibniz made remarkable commitments to combinatorics, including the improvement of the binomial hypothesis.

His work in combinatorics keeps on having applications in different fields, like measurements and software engineering.

2.5. Tact and Legitimate Mastery

Leibniz filled in as a representative and legitimate master, participating in conversations on global regulation.

His strategic endeavors expected to cultivate collaboration among European countries.

The More extensive Effect on Present day Science and Math

3.1. Newton's Heritage

Newton's laws of movement and general attractive energy remain basic standards in physical science.

They give the premise to the investigation of mechanics, divine mechanics, and the comprehension of gravitational powers.

3.2. Leibniz's Documentation

Leibniz's representative documentation for analytics keeps on working with numerical correspondence and articulation.

It works on complex numerical ideas, helping the two mathematicians and researchers.

3.3. Computational Headways

Leibniz's twofold framework fills in as the underpinning of present day figuring and advanced innovation.

It plays had a fundamental impact in the advancement of PCs and data innovation.

3.4. Philosophical Impact

Both Newton's and Leibniz's philosophical commitments have left an enduring effect.

Their thoughts keep on molding conversations in mysticism, epistemology, and the way of thinking of science.

3.5. Moral and Lawful Contemplations

Leibniz's association in lawful and conciliatory undertakings highlights the interdisciplinary idea of his commitments.

His thoughts on global collaboration stay significant in the cutting edge world.

Contemporary Pertinence

4.1. Logical Technique

Newton's principled way to deal with science, portrayed by observational trial and error and numerical meticulousness, stays a foundation of logical philosophy.

His accentuation on the logical strategy keeps on illuminating contemporary logical examination.

4.2. Software engineering

Leibniz's paired framework fills in as the underpinning of current registering, impacting advanced innovation and software engineering.

Propels in computerized innovation owe a huge obligation to his creative reasoning.

4.3. Numerical Documentation

Leibniz's documentation stays key in current arithmetic.

It gives a succinct and strong method for communicating numerical thoughts, improving clearness and accuracy.

4.4. Philosophical Talk

The philosophical thoughts of both Newton and Leibniz keep on motivating contemporary philosophical conversations.

Their commitments to transcendentalism, epistemology, and the way of thinking of science remain subjects of investigation and understanding.

7.2 Newton's laws of motion, universal gravitation, and his impact on physics.

Sir Isaac Newton, a transcending figure throughout the entire existence of science, made fantastic commitments to physical science that changed comprehension we might interpret the actual universe. Newton's three laws of movement and his hypothesis of all inclusive attraction are fundamental rules that keep on forming the field of physical science. This article digs into the importance and ramifications of Newton's regulations and attractive energy hypothesis, featuring their significant effect on material science and the more extensive academic local area.

Newton's Three Laws of Movement

1.1. Newton's Most memorable Regulation: The Law of Latency

Newton's most memorable regulation expresses that an item very still will in general remain very still, and an article moving will in general remain moving except if followed up on by an outside force.

This regulation presented the idea of latency, the property of issue that opposes changes in its condition of movement.

1.2. Newton's Subsequent Regulation: The Law of Power and Speed increase

Newton's subsequent regulation relates the power applied to an article and the subsequent speed increase it encounters.

The law is communicated numerically as F = mama, where F addresses force, m is mass, and an is speed increase.

This regulation gives a quantitative system to understanding how the movement of an item changes because of powers.

1.3. Newton's Third Regulation: The Law of Activity and Response

Newton's third regulation expresses that for each activity, there is an equivalent and inverse response.

This regulation features the guideline of preservation of energy and portrays how powers cooperate between sets of articles.

Widespread Attraction

2.1. The Law of Widespread Attraction

Newton's law of widespread attraction expresses that each mass draws in each and every mass in the universe with a power straightforwardly relative to the result of their masses and contrarily corresponding to the square of the distance between them.

The law is communicated as $F = (G * m_1 * m_2)/r^2$, where F is the gravitational power, G is the widespread gravitational steady, m_1 and m_2 are the majority of the two articles, and r is the distance between their focuses.

This regulation gives a numerical structure to comprehend the power that oversees the movement of divine bodies.

2.2. Influence on Heavenly Mechanics

Newton's hypothesis of all inclusive attractive energy significantly affected divine mechanics.

It made sense of the noticed movement of planets, the moon, and other heavenly bodies, giving a bringing together structure to grasping the planetary group.

2.3. Affirmation through Perception

Newton's law of widespread attraction was affirmed through perceptions, including the precise forecast of planetary circles and the revelation of Neptune in light of gravitational bothers.

Influence on Material science

3.1. The Introduction of Old style Mechanics

Newton's laws of movement established the groundwork for old style mechanics, a part of physical science that portrays the movement of items at ordinary scales.

Traditional mechanics turned into the foundation of physical science for a really long time, giving the structure to figuring out the movement of particles, shots, and frameworks of particles.

3.2. Clarification of Divine Peculiarities

Newton's hypothesis of widespread attractive energy changed the comprehension of heavenly peculiarities.

It made sense of the curved circles of planets, the tides, and the movement of divine articles with phenomenal exactness.

3.3. Improvement of Numerical Physical science

Newton's regulations, communicated in numerical terms, prepared for the advancement of numerical material science.

They showed the force of math as an instrument for understanding and anticipating actual peculiarities.

3.4. Impact on Logical Approach

Newton's accentuation on experimental perception, numerical thoroughness, and the detailing of testable speculations impacted logical approach.

His methodology turned into a model for the logical strategy, underlining the significance of efficient examination.

Inheritance and Contemporary Importance

4.1. Newtonian Physical science in the Advanced World

Newton's laws of movement and widespread attractive energy keep on being major standards in material science.

They are applied in fields like designing, stargazing, and space investigation.

4.2. The Structure for Old style Mechanics

Traditional mechanics, in view of Newton's regulations, stays a fundamental structure for grasping the way of behaving of items in regular daily existence.

It supports designing plan, vehicle elements, and numerous other down to earth applications.

4.3. Constraints and Current Advances

While Newtonian physical science is profoundly exact for most pragmatic purposes, it has impediments in depicting outrageous circumstances, for example, those experienced in relativistic and quantum physical science.

In these areas, Einstein's hypothesis of relativity and quantum mechanics give more exact depictions.

4.4. Continuation of Logical Request

Newton's work epitomizes the continuation of logical request.

His regulations gave an establishment whereupon ensuing ages of physicists fabricated, driving the limits of information further.

7.3Leibniz's work in philosophy, logic, and contributions to various fields.

Gottfried Wilhelm Leibniz, a scholarly goliath of the seventeenth hundred years, was a polymath whose commitments traversed way of thinking, rationale, math, and a wide cluster of disciplines. His work made a permanent imprint on the scholarly scene of his time and keeps on affecting contemporary idea. In this investigation of Leibniz's life and work, we will dig into his huge commitments to theory, rationale, and different fields.

The Life and Setting of Leibniz

Prior to digging into his commitments, understanding the life and setting of Leibniz is fundamental. He was brought into the world on July 1, 1646, in Leipzig, Germany, during a time of colossal scholarly mature. The seventeenth century was set apart by the Logical Upset and the Edification, and Leibniz was at the core of these extraordinary times.

Leibniz got a far reaching schooling in regulation, theory, and math. His initial investigations established the groundwork for his later accomplishments. He was a researcher as well as a negotiator, serving different European courts during his lifetime. These jobs presented him to different scholarly practices and cultivated his interdisciplinary way to deal with information.

Commitments to Theory

Leibniz's philosophical commitments are significant and multi-layered. One of his most huge commitments was the improvement of an extensive powerful framework in light of the standard of "monads." Monads, in Leibniz's way of thinking, are unbreakable, irrelevant, and independent substances that make up the texture of the real world. Every monad has its interesting arrangement of discernments and cravings, making an amicable, pre-laid out concordance among all monads.

This monadology filled in as the supernatural spine of Leibniz's way of thinking, offering a clever point of view on the idea of the real world, cognizance, and the brain body issue. Leibniz contended that the brain and body were particular yet interfaced through pre-laid out amicability, testing the overall Cartesian dualism of his time.

Leibniz's idea of the "best of every single imaginable world" likewise had a massive effect. He suggested that our reality, in spite of its flaws, is all that a big-hearted and transcendent God might have made. This thought affected later scholars and, surprisingly, tracked down its direction into Voltaire's mocking work, "Candide."

In epistemology, Leibniz presented the standard of the "character of indiscernibles," which expresses that assuming two things share overall similar properties, they are indistinguishable. This guideline played a primary job in the improvement of later magical and philosophical idea.

Commitments to Rationale

Leibniz's commitments to rationale are similarly huge. He is credited with concocting the double numeral framework, a central development that underlies present day software engineering. Leibniz's parallel framework, comprising of jus two digits (0 and 1), shaped the premise of every computerized calculation. It was a visionary idea that expected the data age, displaying his capacity to connect reasoning and useful development.

Moreover, Leibniz created formal representative rationale, which prepared for current emblematic rationale and predicate analytics. His documentation framework for legitimate suggestions and connections worked on complex intelligent thinking and made it more available. This advancement altered the investigation of rationale and laid the foundation for the improvement of man-made reasoning and PC programming dialects.

Commitments to Math

Leibniz's numerical commitments are additionally significant. He autonomously created analytics, close by Sir Isaac Newton, however their methodologies varied. Leibniz's documentation for analytics, which utilized the now-natural "d" for separation and "∫" for joining, has turned into the standard documentation in math.

His work in math gave an incredible asset to taking care of issues in material science, designing, and many logical disciplines. It stays a key piece of the numerical toolbox today, representing the getting through effect of his commitments.

Leibniz likewise made commitments to combinatorics, likelihood hypothesis, and number hypothesis. His work on the paired number framework, notwithstanding its sensible ramifications, had pragmatic applications in science and calculation.

Commitments to Science and Innovation

Past his basic commitments to reasoning, rationale, and arithmetic, Leibniz was an early defender of experimentation and the logical technique. He pushed for the methodical assortment of information and exact perception as the reason for logical request. His thoughts affected the improvement of current science and the way of thinking of science.

Leibniz was a productive innovator who planned different machines and gadgets, including a computing machine that could perform math tasks naturally. While a portion of his creations were never underlying his lifetime, they foreshadowed the mechanization and innovation driven universe representing things to come.

Commitments to Law and Discretion

Notwithstanding his work in way of thinking and technical disciplines, Leibniz made critical commitments to statute and tact. He proposed the idea of worldwide regulation as a way to accomplish harmony and collaboration among countries. His discretionary abilities were popular by European courts, where he functioned as a middle person and consultant.

What leibniz would consider a general language for tact, the "characteristica universalis," planned to work with correspondence and common comprehension among countries. While this idea was rarely completely understood, it mirrors his visionary way to deal with taking care of commonsense issues through scholarly development.

Heritage and Impact

Gottfried Wilhelm Leibniz's heritage perseveres in different fields. His philosophical thoughts keep on forming conversations on transcendentalism, epistemology, and morals. In rationale and science, his documentation and ideas remain basic, and his impact on the improvement of the advanced age couldn't possibly be more significant.

Additionally, Leibniz's interdisciplinary way to deal with information, his obligation to reason and orderly reasoning, and his devotion to the quest for truth have left a getting through engrave on the scholarly practice. His commitments act as a demonstration of the force of human creativity and the limit of a solitary person to influence various fields of request.

Chapter 8

Chapter 8

Chapter 8

Cultural and Philosophical Implications

In our quickly globalizing world, the limits that once isolated societies, ways of thinking, and social orders are turning out to be progressively permeable. This interconnectedness has expansive social and philosophical ramifications, reshaping the manner in which we view ourselves, our networks, and the world in general. In this complete investigation, we will dig into the significant ramifications of our interconnected world from both social and philosophical points of view.

Social Ramifications

Social Homogenization versus Variety:

The interconnected world has prompted a juxtaposition of social homogenization and variety. On one hand, the spread of globalized media, innovation, and trade can prompt the disintegration of particular nearby societies. Then again, it has additionally set out open doors for the protection and festivity of social variety as individuals from various foundations come into contact with one another.

Social safeguarding: in light of globalization, numerous networks are effectively attempting to protect their one of a kind social practices and customs. This has led to social celebrations, language rejuvenation endeavors, and a resurgence of native information.

Social combination: Interconnectedness has likewise cultivated social combination, where components from various societies mix to make a novel, new thing. This should be visible in food, craftsmanship, music, and design, as well as the rise of "crossover" characters.

The Force of Social Trade:

Social trade has become more available and boundless because of innovative progressions and expanded worldwide portability. This trade can possibly separate generalizations, advance compassion, and encourage common comprehension among individuals from various foundations.

Training: Instructive trades, concentrate on abroad projects, and internet learning stages permit people to draw in with different societies and thoughts, advancing culturally diverse mindfulness and resilience.

Craftsmanship and Media: The worldwide spread of movies, writing, music, and workmanship opens crowds to new viewpoints and societies, testing assumptions and widening skylines.

Difficulties of Social Apportionment:

While social trade can be advancing, it likewise raises worries about social allotment - the reception of components from one culture by individuals from another, frequently without legitimate comprehension or regard. This has started banters about social responsiveness, regard for customs, and the requirement for informed multifaceted commitment.

Exploring limits: As societies communicate all the more uninhibitedly, people and networks should explore the sensitive harmony among appreciation and apportionment. Regard for social beginnings and open discourse are vital to resolving this issue.

The Job of Language:

Language is both an impression of culture and a driver of social change. In our interconnected world, language assumes a significant part in forming how societies communicate and develop.

Worldwide most widely used language: English has arisen as a worldwide most widely used language for business, tact, and the scholarly community. While this works with correspondence, it can likewise prompt the predominance of one language and the minimization of others.

Language conservation: A few networks are effectively attempting to protect imperiled dialects, remembering them as storehouses of social information and character.

Worldwide Citizenship and Personality:

Interconnectedness has led to a feeling of worldwide citizenship, where people feel associated with the more extensive human local area instead of simply their public or nearby characters. This shift brings up issues about the idea of character and having a place.

Cosmopolitanism: Cosmopolitanism is a philosophical viewpoint that stresses the benefit of being a "resident of the world." It urges people to embrace a more extensive feeling of character and obligation past public boundaries.

Personality emergencies: A few people wrestle with character emergencies despite globalization, as they explore different social, public, and worldwide personalities. This can prompt a feeling of rootlessness or a quest for a steady identity.

Shopper Culture and Realism:

The interconnected world has worked with the worldwide spread of shopper culture and realism. While this has prompted monetary development, it has additionally brought up issues about the effect of commercialization on values, bliss, and the climate.

Industrialism and joy: Philosophical conversations about the connection between material belongings and satisfaction have acquired unmistakable quality. Some contend that the quest for shopper products can take away from additional significant parts of life.

Natural worries: The worldwide creation and conveyance of products have ecological results, bringing up moral issues about supportability and capable utilization.

Philosophical Ramifications

Morals in a Worldwide Setting:

The interconnected world presents new moral difficulties that require philosophical reflection and reaction. Scholars wrestle with inquiries of worldwide equity, common freedoms, and the obligations of people and countries in an interconnected world.

Worldwide equity: The idea of worldwide equity requires the fair dispersion of assets, open doors, and advantages on a worldwide scale. Savants investigate speculations of equity that rise above public limits.

Basic freedoms: The acknowledgment of all inclusive common liberties has turned into a foundation of worldwide morals. Scholars banter the establishments and extent of these privileges in a worldwide setting.

Cosmopolitanism and Ethical constraint:

Cosmopolitanism, as a philosophical point of view, contends that people have ethical constraints to every person, paying little mind to public or social limits. This difficulties customary thoughts of moral obligation in view of closeness or citizenship.

Moral fair-mindedness: Cosmopolitan morals advocate for unbiasedness and contend that ethical commitments ought not be restricted by geology. This has suggestions for issues like worldwide neediness, compassionate mediation, and movement.

Theory of Innovation:

Interconnectedness is intently attached to mechanical progressions. Logicians dive into the moral and powerful components of innovation, scrutinizing its effect on human life, independence, and importance.

Mechanical determinism: A few thinkers investigate the possibility that innovation shapes human qualities and ways of behaving, prompting inquiries concerning organization and control in an interconnected world.

Existential inquiries: The quick improvement of innovation has brought up existential issues about the idea of humankind, the limits among people and machines, and the importance of life in a computerized age.

Epistemology and Truth in the Data Age:

The computerized upset and the accessibility of data readily available have tested conventional ideas of information and truth. Logicians wrestle with inquiries regarding the unwavering quality of data, the idea of truth, and the job of mastery.

Data over-burden: The wealth of data presents difficulties in distinctive solid sources from deception and disinformation. Logicians talk about procedures for decisive reasoning and epistemic obligation.

Post-truth time: The interconnected world has led to a "post-truth" period, described by the obscuring of realities and feelings. Logicians investigate the ramifications of this peculiarity for public talk and a majority rule government.

Existentialism and Significance in a Divided World:

Existentialist way of thinking, which frequently centers around individual presence and opportunity, takes on new aspects in an interconnected world. Logicians consider inquiries of legitimacy, distance, and the quest for importance in a world portrayed by intricacy and vulnerability.

Credibility and estrangement: The interconnected world can prompt a feeling of disengagement and distance. Existentialist way of thinking urges people to go up against these sentiments and look for legitimacy in their decisions and activities.

Significance and reason: Logicians investigate the mission for importance and reason in reality as we know it where customary strict and social systems may never again give replies. Existentialist idea offers bits of knowledge into tracking down importance even with existential inquiries.

Morals of Computerized reasoning and Advanced Presence:

As innovation progresses, thinkers wrestle with moral inquiries encompassing man-made reasoning (simulated intelligence) and computerized presence. Points incorporate simulated intelligence morals, computerized security, and the ethical status of man-made intelligence elements.

Man-made intelligence morals: The turn of events and utilization of simulated intelligence bring up moral issues about liability, responsibility, and the treatment of simulated intelligence frameworks. Rationalists banter the ethical status of man-made intelligence substances and the potential for artificial intelligence to show moral organization.

Computerized security and character: The advanced age has led to worries about protection, observation, and the commodification of individual information. Savants investigate the ramifications of advanced presence for ideas of character and independence.

8.1 The calculus controversy's cultural and philosophical implications.

The analytics contention, frequently alluded to as the "need debate" between Sir Isaac Newton and Gottfried Wilhelm Leibniz, is a generally huge episode in the improvement of math. Past its numerical angles, this question had expansive social and philosophical ramifications that keep on resounding in the realm of science, reasoning, and scholarly talk. In this exposition, we will investigate the math contention and its significant social and philosophical ramifications.

The Beginnings of the Math Contention

The analytics debate arose in the late seventeenth century when both Newton and Leibniz freely fostered the underpinnings of what might become math. In spite of the fact that their methodologies were unique, the two men made momentous commitments to this new field of science.

Newton, an English mathematician and physicist, fostered his technique for "the analytics" during the 1660s and 1670s. He utilized the idea of fluxions, which included thinking about minuscule changes in amounts after some time, to tackle issues connected with movement and change. Notwithstanding, his work was introduced in a profoundly cryptic and hazy way.

Leibniz, a German polymath, fostered his own arrangement of math freely around a similar time. He presented the now-natural documentation for separation (dy/dx) and joining ($\int$) and laid out the central standards of math. Leibniz's documentation and strategy were more open and straightforward than Newton's, which added to the far reaching reception of his methodology.

The Contention Unfurls

The contention came to public consideration in the mid eighteenth hundred years, as both Newton and Leibniz's work acquired unmistakable quality. What started as a logical debate before long swelled into a nationalistic and individual contention, with English mathematicians supporting Newton and Mainland European mathematicians leaning toward Leibniz. This social setting added layers of intricacy to the debate.

Social Ramifications

Patriotism and Logical Need:

The analytics contention became entwined with patriotism, especially among Britain and the Mainland. English mathematicians considered Newton to be their public legend not entirely settled to guard his need in the improvement of analytics. Then again, Leibniz was hailed as a German scholarly light, and his allies underlined his commitments.

Public pride: The debate featured the job of logical accomplishment in supporting public pride and personality. The possibility of one's nation creating a progressive numerical idea was a wellspring of esteem.

Contention and rivalry: The competition among Britain and the Mainland heightened the debate, on occasion eclipsing the numerical benefits of the case. This highlights how social variables can impact the course of scholarly discussions.

Language and Documentation:

Leibniz's documentation and way to deal with math were more open and easy to understand than Newton's. This semantic and notational part of the discussion has social ramifications, as it mirrors the job of language and imagery in forming scholarly talk.

Lucidity and openness: Leibniz's documentation was intended all things considered and compact, making math more available to a more extensive crowd. This approach lined up with Illumination goals of making information accessible to all.

Correspondence and scattering: Leibniz's documentation added to the fast spread of analytics across Europe. It turned into the most widely used language of science, underlining the job of language in the spread of thoughts.

Philosophical Ramifications

Epistemology and Procedure:

The analytics contention brought up significant issues about the idea of numerical information and the techniques used to gain it.

Strategic pluralism: The discussion featured the presence of various legitimate techniques for tackling numerical issues. This difficulties the thought of a solitary "right" way to deal with information.

Induction versus Logic: Newton's methodology was established in a more empiricist custom, underlining perceptions and actual standards. Leibniz's methodology, then again, mirrored a pragmatist theory that zeroed in on dynamic thinking and representative documentation. This differentiation highlighted the philosophical strains among observation and realism.

Effect on Way of thinking of Science:

The math contention lastingly affected the way of thinking of math, impacting ensuing conversations on numerical approach and the groundworks of arithmetic.

Foundationalism and formalism: The question added to banters about the groundworks of science. Mathematicians and thinkers investigated inquiries regarding the proverbial premise of arithmetic and the connection between formal frameworks and numerical reality.

Instinct and thoroughness: The contention brought up issues about the job of instinct and meticulousness in arithmetic. Mathematicians wrestled with the need to offset natural bits of knowledge with formal verifications, a subject that endures in contemporary conversations on numerical practice.

Truth and Objectivity:

The analytics contention additionally addressed more extensive philosophical inquiries regarding the idea of truth and objectivity in science.

Objective information: The debate showed the way that numerical bits of insight could be found freely by various people utilizing various strategies. This featured the objectivity of numerical information, which isn't dependent upon individual viewpoints.

Verifiable viewpoint: From a verifiable stance, the discussion highlighted the developing and dynamic nature of numerical information. It demonstrated the way that numerical thoughts and documentations can foster after some time and adjust to changing scholarly settings.

Heritage and Examples:

The analytics discussion at last didn't take away from the meaning of the numerical commitments of Newton and Leibniz. The two men made significant and enduring commitments to analytics, and their work keeps on being central in math and science.

Congruity in variety: The contention's goal represents the limit of different strategies and documentations to coincide inside a field of study. It fills in as an update that variety in approaches can improve the advancement of information.

Cooperation and transparency: The analytics debate features the significance of open correspondence and coordinated effort in the progression of information. It is a useful example about the possible traps of mystery and competition in scholarly pursuits.

8.2 The contrast between Newton's empiricism and Leibniz's rationalism.

The seventeenth century denoted a critical period throughout the entire existence of reasoning and science, with two transcending figures, Sir Isaac Newton and Gottfried Wilhelm Leibniz, making enduring commitments to the two fields. What recognizes their methodologies and ways of thinking are their generally unique epistemological positions: Newton's induction and Leibniz's logic. In this paper, we will dive into the center principles of these two differentiating philosophical frameworks, looking at how they molded the idea and work of these famous scholars and their effect on the improvement of science and reasoning.

Newton's Observation

Observation is a philosophical position that stresses the significance of tangible experience as the groundwork of information. It sets that how we might interpret the world is gotten from our tactile discernments and that experimental proof is the reason for making claims about the real world. Newton, an English mathematician and physicist, was an unmistakable defender of induction. His observational methodology is most apparent in his amazing work, the "Philosophiæ Naturalis Principia Mathematica" (frequently alluded to just as the "Principia"), where he formed the laws of movement and widespread attractive energy.

Perception and Trial and error:

Newton's exact way of thinking is exemplified by his dependence on perception and trial and error. His laws of movement and the law of widespread attractive energy were formed in light of cautious perceptions of heavenly and earthly peculiarities. For example, his examination of the movement of the moon and the planets required fastidious cosmic perceptions.

Logical strategy: Newton's accentuation on precise perception and trial and error turned into a foundation of the logical technique. His work established the groundwork for exact science, where speculations are tried through thorough trial and error and perception.

Inductive Thinking:

Newton's experimentation was firmly connected to inductive thinking, a technique for intelligent derivation that gets general standards from explicit perceptions. His laws of movement and widespread attraction were inductive in nature, as they summed up from experimental information to form general standards.

General regulations from explicit examples: Newton's progress in figuring out broad regulations from explicit cases epitomizes the force of inductive thinking. His regulations gave a brought together structure to making sense of different actual peculiarities.

Protection from Speculations Without Observational Help:

Newton was profoundly careful about proposing speculations without observational help. He broadly avoided estimating about the reason for gravitational fascination past portraying its numerical way of behaving. He stuck to the view that logical clarifications ought to be immovably grounded in experimental proof.

Systemic limitation: Newton's hesitance to participate in speculative clarifications highlights his obligation to experimentation and his confidence in the requirement for a solid exact starting point for logical cases.

Exact Underpinning of Arithmetic:

Newton's experimentation additionally stretched out to arithmetic, where he fostered the technique for "the analytics" (presently known as differential and essential math) to take care of issues in science and physical science. His work in analytics was solidly established in the examination of genuine peculiarities.

Science as an instrument: For Newton, math was a useful asset for depicting and breaking down the observational world. His improvement of analytics gave a numerical language to portraying change and movement.

Leibniz's Realism

Realism, rather than experimentation, stresses the job of reason, mind, and natural information in gaining information. It places that specific bits of insight can be known autonomously of tactile experience using reason and scholarly knowledge. Leibniz, a German scholar, mathematician, and polymath, was a main figure in logic, and his way of thinking is typified in his popular work, the "Monadology."

Natural Thoughts and Deduced Information:

Leibniz's logic sets the presence of natural thoughts and deduced information, recommending that specific insights are intrinsic in the human psyche and can be known freely of tactile experience. He contended that the brain contains natural ideas that are initiated and created through reason.

Supernatural insights: Leibniz trusted that mystical bits of insight, for example, the guideline of non-inconsistency and the rule of adequate explanation, were not gotten from tactile experience however were known deduced through normal reflection.

The Guideline of Adequate Explanation:

Fundamental to Leibniz's logic is the guideline of adequate explanation, which declares that all that occurs or exists has an adequate justification for why it is for all intents and purposes and not in any case. This rule supports Leibniz's powerful framework and his confidence in an amicable and reasonable universe.

A powerful perspective: Leibniz's obligation to the rule of adequate explanation mirrored his pragmatist reasoning and drove him to foster a complete magical framework that looked to make sense of the idea of the real world, causation, and presence.

Sane Systematization of Information:

Leibniz was known for his endeavors to arrange information using legitimate and numerical documentation. His improvement of the characteristica universalis, an all inclusive language or representative framework for addressing ideas and information, exemplified his realist way to deal with sorting out and figuring out data.

The quest for a general language: Leibniz's characteristica universalis meant to make a sensible and efficient language that could act as an establishment for all human information. This mirrors his pragmatist confidence in the force of motivation to make a bound together procedure for understanding.

Supernatural Confidence and Theodicy:
Leibniz's logic reached out to his philosophical reflections on mystical idealism and theodicy. He accepted that the universe was portrayed by the "best of every single imaginable world" and that the presence of shrewd and enduring could be accommodated with a considerate and normal divinity.

An agreeable perspective: Leibniz's logic permitted him to build a powerful structure in which the clear inconsistencies of the world could be settled through reason. His theodicy, while questionable, addressed an endeavor to accommodate confidence and reason.

Looking at Newton's Experimentation and Leibniz's Logic Epistemological Establishments:
Newton (Experimentation): Newton's epistemological establishment was established in tangible experience and observational proof. He accentuated the significance of perception and trial and error in securing information.

Leibniz (Realism): Leibniz's epistemology depended on reason and the confidence in natural thoughts and deduced information. He contended that specific insights could be known autonomously of tactile experience.

Way to deal with Arithmetic and Science:
Newton (Experimentation): Newton's way to deal with math and science was exact, grounded in the examination of actual peculiarities. He created analytics to tackle certifiable issues.

Leibniz (Logic): Leibniz's way to deal with math and science was rationalistic, with math seen as an instrument for depicting and coordinating information. He created math utilizing a more theoretical and representative methodology.

Mystical Convictions:
Newton (Experimentation): Newton's supernatural convictions were less articulated in his logical work, and he frequently abstained from hypothesizing about a definitive reasons for regular peculiarities.

Leibniz (Logic): Leibniz's realism drove him to foster an exhaustive mystical framework that looked to make sense of the idea of the real world, causation, and presence. His work reached out into the domain of philosophy and theodicy.

The Job of Imagery and Documentation:

Newton (Induction): Newton's numerical documentation and imagery were less efficient and conceptual contrasted with Leibniz's. He utilized math basically as a device for taking care of commonsense issues.

Leibniz (Realism): Leibniz's improvement of the characteristica universalis mirrored his pragmatist want to make an orderly and emblematic language for sorting out and addressing information.

Relationship to the Illumination:

Newton (Induction): Newton's exact methodology lined up with the Edification's accentuation on experimental perception, trial and error, and the quest for regular regulations.

Leibniz (Realism): Leibniz's logic, while persuasive, didn't adjust as intimately with the Illumination's accentuation on observation and secularism. His mystical and theodical sees in some cases set him in strain with Edification thought.

Philosophical Ramifications of the Differentiation

Epistemological Variety: The Newton-Leibniz contrast outlines the variety of epistemological methodologies inside way of thinking and science. It shows that there are various substantial approaches to getting information, going from exact perception to normal allowance.

Similarity: The difference challenges the idea that experimentation and logic are totally unrelated. While Newton and Leibniz represent various closures of the range, their work

likewise demonstrates the way that these methodologies can be viable, for however long they are utilized wisely.

The Job of Reasoning in Science: The difference brings up issues about the job of reasoning in science. Newton's exact

methodology inclined more in the direction of logical practice, while Leibniz's realism stretched out into otherworldly
and philosophical inquiries. This shows the crossing point of
reasoning and science.

Social and Verifiable Setting: The differentiating approaches mirror the social and authentic settings in which
Newton and Leibniz lived and worked. Newton's experimentation lined up with the Illumination's accentuation on exact
perception, while Leibniz's realism was well established in th

**8.3How the dispute reflected broader intellectual trends
of the time.**

The Newton-Leibniz disagreement regarding the innovation
of analytics was in excess of a numerical fight; it was an
impression of the more extensive scholarly and philosophical
flows of the late seventeenth and mid eighteenth hundreds
of years. To comprehend the meaning of this question, one
should think about the scholarly milieu of the period, described by the Illumination, the Logical Unrest, and the rise
of groundbreaking thoughts regarding information, authority,
and the quest for truth. In this article, we will investigate what
the analytics contention reflected and meant for these more
extensive scholarly patterns of the time.

1. **The Illumination and the Time of Reason**
   The late seventeenth and mid eighteenth hundreds of
   years were set apart by the Illumination, a scholarly development that commended reason, induction, and the
   quest for information as a way to advance and human
   improvement. Illumination scholars upheld for the utilization of motivation to challenge custom, notion, and
   laid out power.
   The Question's Appearance:
   Observation versus Realism: The debate set Newton's
   exact methodology in opposition to Leibniz's rationalistic

strategy. This difference featured the continuous discussion between induction, which underscored the significance of tangible experience, and realism, which focused on reason and natural thoughts as wellsprings of information.

Straightforwardness and Lucidity: Leibniz's documentation and way to deal with math were more straightforward and easy to use than Newton's. This lines up with the

Illumination's accentuation on clear and open correspondence of information, making complex thoughts justifiable to a more extensive crowd.

Spread of Information: The discussion drew the consideration of Edification scholarly people, who considered it to be an illustration of the force of reason and scholarly discussion. It added to the spread of logical information and the possibility that scholarly questions could prompt advancement.

2. **The Logical Insurgency and Experimental Request**

The Logical Transformation, which had its foundations in the sixteenth 100 years, kept on profoundly shaping scholarly idea during the math debate. It underscored exact request, trial and error, and the advancement of methodical techniques for grasping the normal world.

The Question's Appearance:

Logical Technique: The analytics debate delineated the significance of deliberate perception and trial and error, signs of the logical strategy. Newton's and Leibniz's work depended on observational proof and inductive thinking, lining up with the standards of the Logical Insurgency.

Science as an Instrument for Grasping Nature: Both Newton and Leibniz considered math to be an integral asset for figuring out the regular world. Their commitments to analytics mirrored a more extensive pattern in which math assumed an undeniably focal part in logical request.

Widespread Standards: The quest for general standards and regulations, a vital part of the Logical Transformation, was clear in the math debate. Both Newton and Leibniz tried to plan general regulations that could make sense of a large number of regular peculiarities.

3. **The Changing Idea of Scholarly Power**

The math discussion happened during a period when customary wellsprings of scholarly power, like the congregation and laid out doctrine, were being tested. The question mirrored a shift toward esteeming individual scholarly commitments and cultivating a feeling of scholarly freedom.

The Debate's Appearance:

Autonomous Learned people: Newton and Leibniz were both free masterminds who fostered their thoughts beyond formal intellectual or institutional settings. This featured

the developing impact of individual researchers and their capacity to challenge laid out power.

Protected innovation and Proprietorship: The debate likewise brought up issues about licensed innovation and responsibility for. It mirrored a more extensive pattern in which the possession and spread of information were turning out to be progressively significant issues.

Scholarly VIP: The discussion raised Newton and Leibniz to the situation with scholarly superstars, with their thoughts and commitments firmly followed and bantered by researchers and people in general. This mirrored a developing interest in the lives and thoughts of individual scholars.

4. **The Job of Correspondence and Print Culture**

The analytics question harmonized with the multiplication of print culture and the spread of thoughts through books, leaflets, and diaries. This period saw the ascent of logical social orders, institutes, and organizations of correspondence that worked with the trading of information.

The Debate's Appearance:

Dispersal of Thoughts: The question was generally announced through distributions, letters, and discussions. This mirrored the developing significance of scattering logical and philosophical plans to a more extensive crowd.

Logical Social orders and Organizations: Newton and Leibniz were the two individuals from logical social orders and had broad organizations of reporters. These organizations assumed a part in forming the course of the debate and featured the cooperative idea of scholarly request.

Public Commitment: The question connected with a more extensive public crowd, including those external the scholar and mainstream researchers. This mirrored a developing interest in science and math among the informed public.

5. **The Quest for All inclusiveness and Stupendous Blends**

The math debate happened in a scholarly environment portrayed by a mission for comprehensiveness and excellent unions. Researchers tried to reveal fundamental rules that could make sense of a great many peculiarities and make bound together frameworks of information.

The Question's Appearance:

General Standards: Both Newton and Leibniz tried to form all inclusive rules that could make sense of the movement of heavenly bodies as well as a large group of other regular peculiarities. This mirrored the more extensive longing for a brought together comprehension of the normal world.

Philosophical Frameworks: Leibniz, specifically, was known for his endeavors to develop exhaustive philosophical frameworks that could represent supernatural, moral, and logical inquiries inside a solitary structure. The question assumed a part in these more extensive scholarly undertakings.

Chapter 9

The Legacy of The Calculus Controversy

The math contention, a verifiable question between Sir Isaac Newton and Gottfried Wilhelm Leibniz over the development and need of analytics, left a getting through inheritance that reaches out a long ways past the domain of math. This contention, which crossed the late seventeenth and mid eighteenth hundreds of years, molded the advancement of analytics as well as had significant social, philosophical, and verifiable ramifications. In this thorough investigation, we will dive into the rich tradition of the analytics contention and its sweeping effect on math, science, reasoning, and the more extensive scholarly scene.

The Introduction of Analytics

Prior to digging into the tradition of the contention, understanding the introduction of math and the commitments of Newton and Leibniz is fundamental. The two mathematicians fostered their ways to deal with analytics autonomously, and keeping in mind that their documentations and techniques contrasted, their work established the groundwork for this progressive part of math.

Newton's Commitment:

Newton's work on analytics, as exemplified in his "Philosophiæ Naturalis Principia Mathematica" (the Principia), was portrayed by his technique for "the math." He utilized the idea of "fluxions" and "the strategy for first and last proportions" to examine paces of progress and movement.

Newton's methodology, be that as it may, was introduced in a clandestine and dark way, utilizing mathematical strategies and restricted documentation. His hesitance to distribute exhaustive deals with math in an opportune style added to the debate.

Leibniz's Commitment:

Leibniz, a German polymath, fostered his own arrangement of math freely. He presented the now-natural documentation for separation (dy/dx) and mix ($\int$) and laid out the crucial standards of analytics.

Leibniz's documentation and technique were more open and straightforward than Newton's, prompting the far and wide reception of his methodology.

In view of this establishment, we can now investigate the getting through tradition of the math contention.

Arithmetic and the Tradition of the Analytics Debate

The analytics discussion prodded endeavors to formalize the underpinnings of math thoroughly. Mathematicians like Augustin-Louis Cauchy and Karl Weierstrass in the nineteenth century fostered the idea of cutoff points and gave a strong numerical supporting to analytics.

The tradition of the discussion is the improvement of genuine investigation, a part of science that gives a thorough structure to math and the investigation of genuine numbers.

Leibniz's Documentation and the Normalization of Math:

Leibniz's documentation for separation and mix became standard in math because of its lucidity and utility. It took into consideration a more succinct and expressive portrayal of numerical thoughts.

Today, Leibniz's documentation stays an indispensable piece of analytics and numerical talk, making the subject more open to understudies and scientists the same.

Joining of Analytics into Math Educational plan:

The goal of the analytics contention, with both Newton and Leibniz perceived for their commitments, prompted the acknowledgment and mix of analytics into the science educational program.

Analytics is presently an essential part of math instruction, educated at both optional and tertiary levels, and fills in as the doorway to higher math and sciences.

Science and the Tradition of the Math Contention

Math, as evolved by Newton and Leibniz, assumed a vital part in the headway of physical science and designing. It gave the numerical devices to portray and dissect actual peculiarities, prompting forward leaps in mechanics, optics, and stargazing.

Newton's laws of movement and widespread attraction, which depended vigorously on math, established the groundwork for old style physical science.

Mechanical Advancement:

The tradition of the math debate stretches out to mechanical advancement. Analytics is fundamental for the improvement of advances going from the development of extensions and high rises to the plan of airplane and shuttle.

It underlies the fields of software engineering, information examination, and man-made reasoning, forming the mechanical scene of the cutting edge world.

Logical Approach and Experimental Request:

The analytics discussion exemplified the significance of exact perception, trial and error, and efficient request in logical philosophy. Both Newton and Leibniz depended on observational proof and inductive thinking to foster their thoughts.

This heritage keeps on advising the work on regarding science, stressing the job of observational proof in speculation testing and hypothesis improvement.

Reasoning and the Tradition of the Analytics Discussion

The analytics discussion brought up philosophical issues about the idea of information and the strategies for getting it. It featured the difference between Newton's experimentation and Leibniz's logic.

This heritage reaches out to progressing banters in epistemology, where scholars investigate the jobs of tactile experience, reason, and instinct in the securing of information.

Reasoning of Math:

The debate affected the way of thinking of math, with suggestions for inquiries concerning the underpinnings of science, numerical truth, and the connection between numerical articles and the actual world.

Logicians have analyzed the tradition of the debate in conversations about numerical documentation, meticulousness, and the idea of numerical ideas.

Transcendentalism and the Idea of The real world:

Leibniz's logic and his investigation of supernatural ideas, like monads and the standard of adequate explanation, were impacted by the math contention.

This heritage stretches out to contemporary conversations in power, where scholars investigate inquiries concerning the idea of the real world, causation, and the guideline of adequate explanation.

Social and Verifiable Effect

The analytics discussion raised both Newton and Leibniz to the situation with logical superstars. Their commitments and the actual question turned out to be important for the social portrayal of science and math.

The tradition of the debate incorporates the public's interest with logical virtuoso and the human show behind scholarly accomplishments.

Patriotism and Scholarly Personality:

The debate had nationalistic suggestions, with English mathematicians supporting Newton and Mainland European mathematicians inclining toward Leibniz.

The tradition of the debate features the crossing point of public personality, scholarly contention, and the quest for logical acknowledgment.

Historiography and Authentic Strategy

The goal of the math debate relied upon itemized documentation and the assessment of verifiable records, including letters, compositions, and distributed works.

The tradition of the debate stresses the significance of authentic examination and chronicled work in grasping the advancement of science and arithmetic.

Verifiable Setting and Scholarly Patterns:

The math discussion highlights the meaning of putting verifiable occasions in their more extensive scholarly, social, and political setting.

History specialists of science and arithmetic keep on investigating the authentic setting of logical turns of events, drawing on the tradition of the question.

9.1 Summarizing the enduring significance of the Newton vs. Leibniz calculus controversy.

The Newton versus Leibniz math debate, which seethed in the late seventeenth and mid eighteenth hundreds of years, has made a permanent imprint on the fields of math, science, reasoning, and the more extensive scholarly scene. While the actual question was established in a numerical fight over the development and need of math, its getting through importance rises above the universe of numbers and conditions. In this rundown, we will distil the persevering through significance of this authentic episode into central issues that feature its effect on different spaces of human information and attempt.

1. **Primary Effect on Math:**
   The analytics discussion prodded the advancement of thorough numerical investigation. Mathematicians in the nineteenth hundred years, like Augustin-Louis Cauchy and Karl Weierstrass, based upon the debate's heritage by giving a strong groundwork to analytics, including the idea of cutoff points and exact meanings of subsidiary and fundamental.
   Leibniz's documentation for separation and reconciliation turned into the norm in math because of its lucidity and utility. This documentation stays being used today and fills in as a demonstration of the question's getting through impact on numerical correspondence.
   The math discussion prompted the coordination of analytics into the science educational program, making it an essential part of training. It fills in as the doorway to higher math and logical disciplines, guaranteeing that people in the future keep on profiting from the question's numerical heritage.

2. **Change of Logical Request:**
   Math, as evolved by Newton and Leibniz, assumed a vital part in propelling physical science, designing, and the innate sciences. It gave the fundamental numerical instruments to portraying, investigating, and anticipating actual peculiarities.
   The tradition of the debate stretches out to mechanical advancement, impacting fields as different as structural designing, aviation, software engineering, and computerized reasoning. Analytics supports current innovations and logical headways, forming the contemporary world.
   The math discussion exemplified the significance of

exact perception, trial and error, and efficient request in logical philosophy. Both Newton and Leibniz depended on exact proof and inductive thinking, building up the primary standards of observational science.

3. **Philosophical Reflections on Information and Reality:**
   The debate brought up significant philosophical issues about the idea of information and the strategies for gaining it. It highlighted the differentiation between Newton's induction, which stressed tactile experience, and Leibniz's realism, which focused on reason and natural thoughts.

   The tradition of the question perseveres in continuous discussions in epistemology, where scholars keep on investigating the jobs of tactile experience, reason, and instinct in the securing of information. It stays a reference point for conversations on the idea of human comprehension.

   The analytics discussion affected the way of thinking of science, with suggestions for inquiries concerning the groundworks of arithmetic, numerical truth, and the connection between numerical items and the actual world. Rationalists have analyzed the question's heritage in conversations about numerical documentation, meticulousness, and the idea of numerical ideas.

4. **Social Portrayal and Logical Superstar:**
   The contention raised both Newton and Leibniz to the situation with logical superstars. Their commitments and the show encompassing the question turned out to be essential for the social portrayal of science and math.

   The tradition of the question reaches out to the public's interest with logical virtuoso and the human stories behind scholarly accomplishments. It keeps on forming the manner in which society sees and celebrates logical accomplishment.

5. **Patriotism and Scholarly Personality:**
The debate had nationalistic suggestions, with English mathematicians supporting Newton and Mainland European mathematicians leaning toward Leibniz. It mirrored the convergence of public character, scholarly contention, and the quest for logical acknowledgment.
The tradition of the question features the job of public character and pride throughout the entire existence of science. It fills in as a sign of how social and political variables can impact the course of scholarly discussions.
6. **Historiography and Authentic Technique:**

The goal of the math discussion depended on itemized documentation, chronicled research, and the assessment of verifiable records, including letters, compositions, and distributed works. This philosophy has turned into a sign of the investigation of the historical backdrop of science and math.

The tradition of the question highlights the significance of putting authentic occasions in their more extensive scholarly, social, and political setting. Students of history of science and math keep on investigating the authentic setting of logical turns of events, drawing on the examples of the question.

9.2 Reflecting on how their rivalry advanced mathematics and science.

The contention between Sir Isaac Newton and Gottfried Wilhelm Leibniz, fixated on the development and need of analytics, was a verifiable debate as well as an impetus for critical headways in math and science. This serious scholarly rivalry, spreading over the late seventeenth and mid eighteenth hundreds of years, prodded the two mathematicians to push the limits of information and established the groundwork for weighty improvements in their particular fields. In this reflection, we will investigate how the competition among Newton and Leibniz progressed math and science, leaving a significant and getting through heritage.

1. **The Introduction of Analytics: Free however Concurrent Turn of events**

   One of the most wonderful parts of the contention is the free yet concurrent advancement of math by Newton and Leibniz. The two mathematicians moved toward the subject with one of a kind points of view, documentations, and philosophies, and their work laid the basis for this progressive part of math.

   Newton's Methodology: Newton's technique for "the math" depended on the idea of "fluxions" and "the strategy for first and last proportions." His methodology was fundamentally mathematical, and he utilized minuscule amounts to examine paces of progress and movement.

   Leibniz's Methodology: Leibniz, then again, presented the now-natural documentation for separation (dy/dx) and incorporation ($\int$) and figured out the crucial standards of analytics. His documentation and strategy were more straightforward and open than Newton's, prompting their boundless reception.

2. **Advancement of Thorough Numerical Investigation**

   Idea of Cutoff points: In the nineteenth hundred years, mathematicians, for example, Augustin-Louis Cauchy and Karl Weierstrass fostered the idea of cutoff points, which gave a thorough premise to math. This idea resolved the issue of infinitesimals and vulnerabilities that had been available in the early details of analytics.

   Exact Definitions: The competition provoked mathematicians to give exact meanings of subsidiary and basic, disposing of ambiguities and guaranteeing numerical thoroughness. This work added to the improvement of genuine investigation, a part of math that supports analytics.

3. Normalization of Math Documentation
   Availability: Leibniz's documentation made analytics more open and easy to understand. It took into consideration a more brief and expressive portrayal of numerical thoughts, working with both instructing and research.
   Worldwide Reception: Leibniz's documentation is still being used today, and it has turned into a necessary piece of numerical talk around the world. Mathematicians, researchers, and specialists depend on this documentation to impart and take care of complicated issues.

4. Joining into the Science Educational program
   Crucial Part: Analytics turned into an essential part of math schooling, educated at both optional and tertiary levels. It fills in as a primary subject that opens ways to higher math and sciences.
   Entryway to Higher Learning: Analytics is viewed as the doorway to cutting edge numerical and logical disciplines. It is an essential for fields like physical science, designing, financial matters, and software engineering.

5. Progressions in Physical science and Designing
   Newton's Laws of Movement and Attractive energy: Newton's work on math, as exemplified in his "Philosophiæ Naturalis Principia Mathematica" (the Principia), assumed a focal part in figuring out his laws of movement and the law of general attractive energy. These regulations, in view of analytics, established the groundwork for traditional physical science.
   Innovative Advancement: The tradition of the contention stretches out to mechanical advancement. Analytics is fundamental for the advancement of innovations going from the development of scaffolds and high rises to the plan of airplane and space apparatus. It is a crucial

instrument for specialists and researchers across different disciplines.

6. **Logical Technique and Experimental Request**
Experimental Establishment: Both Newton and Leibniz depended on observational proof and inductive thinking in their work. Newton's investigation of divine and earthbound peculiarities, as well as Leibniz's investigation of numerical and actual issues, exhibited the observational premise of their commitments.

Logical Technique: The contention supported the logical strategy, stressing the methodical testing of speculations through experimental proof. This technique stays a foundation of logical request, directing specialists in their quest for information.

7. **Philosophical Reflections on Information and Reality**
Epistemological Request: The question highlighted the difference between Newton's observation, which stressed tactile experience, and Leibniz's logic, which focused on reason and intrinsic thoughts. It provoked philosophical reflections on the jobs of tactile experience, reason, and instinct in the procurement of information.

Reasoning of Arithmetic: The debate impacted the way of thinking of math, with suggestions for inquiries regarding the groundworks of science, numerical truth, and the connection between numerical articles and the actual world. Thinkers have analyzed the debate's heritage in conversations about numerical documentation, meticulousness, and the idea of numerical ideas.

8. **Social Portrayal and Logical Superstar**
Social Effect: The contention and the commitments of Newton and Leibniz turned out to be important for the social portrayal of science and math. Their names became inseparable from scholarly virtuoso and accomplishment.

Public Interest: The tradition of the contention perseveres in the public's interest with logical virtuoso and the human stories behind scholarly accomplishments. It has added to the famous impression of researchers as people who shape the course of human information.

9. Patriotism and Scholarly Character

Public Pride: The debate set English mathematicians on the side of Newton in opposition to Mainland European mathematicians inclining toward Leibniz. It featured the job of public pride and character throughout the entire existence of science.

Scholarly Personality: The competition additionally molded the scholarly character of countries and areas. It fills in as a verifiable illustration of how social and political elements can impact the course of scholarly discussions.

10. Historiography and Authentic Philosophy

Verifiable Exploration: The competition highlighted the significance of authentic examination in grasping the improvement of science and math. It underscored the requirement for cautious assessment of essential sources, including letters, compositions, and distributed works.

Relevant Examination: The tradition of the contention features the meaning of setting authentic occasions in their more extensive scholarly, social, and political setting. Students of history of science and arithmetic keep on investigating the verifiable setting of logical turns of events, drawing on the examples of the competition.

9.3 The continued relevance of their contributions in contemporary mathematics.

The commitments of Sir Isaac Newton and Gottfried Wilhelm Leibniz to arithmetic, especially their improvement of analytics, keep on being exceptionally significant and essential in contemporary science. Regardless of the hundreds of years that have passed since their work, the ideas, documentations, and strategies they presented stay fundamental in different numerical teaches and have tracked down applications in assorted fields. In this investigation, we will dig into the proceeded with significance of Newton and Leibniz's commitments in contemporary arithmetic.

1. The Principal Ideas of Analytics

One of the most getting through traditions of Newton and Leibniz is the central ideas of math they presented. These ideas support many parts of arithmetic and have become
fundamental instruments for understanding and taking care of perplexing issues. Here are a few vital parts of math that remain profoundly pertinent today:

Limits: The idea of cutoff points, which arose as a method for figuring out imperceptibly little amounts, is central in math. It permits mathematicians to thoroughly characterize subsidiaries and integrals, framing the premise of genuine examination. Limits are integral to the investigation of progression, assembly, and the way of behaving of capabilities.

Subsidiaries: The thought of subordinates, presented by both Newton and Leibniz freely, stays a foundation of math. Subordinates measure paces of progress and give fundamental devices to enhancement, bend portraying, and tackling differential conditions. They have applications in physical science, designing, financial aspects, and science.

Integrals: Integrals, which address the collection of amounts, are one more key idea in math. They are utilized to figure regions, volumes, and different types of gathering. Strategies of combination, like reconciliation by parts and halfway portions, are key in tackling complex numerical and actual issues.

Principal Hypothesis of Math: The Central Hypothesis of Analytics, created by both Newton and Leibniz, lays out a major association among separation and combination. It stays a bedrock standard in math and assumes an essential part in genuine examination.

2. Standard Documentation for Math

Leibniz's Documentation: Leibniz's documentation for separation (dy/dx) and joining ($\int$) is broadly embraced in contemporary science. It gives a brief and natural portrayal of numerical thoughts, making it simpler for mathematicians to communicate and convey complex ideas.

dx and dy: The utilization of "dx" and "dy" as differentials, an idea firmly connected with Leibniz, stays an essential piece of math. These differentials are fundamental in characterizing subsidiaries and integrals and assume a vital part in math based courses.

3. Multivariate Analytics and Vector Investigation

Halfway Subordinates: The idea of fractional subsidiaries, an expansion of standard subsidiaries to elements of various factors, is a vital improvement of multivariate math. It

is critical in enhancement, the investigation of surfaces and bends in three-layered space, and the plan of fractional differential conditions.

Vector Analytics: Vector math, which incorporates ideas like inclinations, uniqueness, and twist, stretches out the standards of analytics to vector fields. These ideas are utilized broadly in material science, especially in the investigation of electromagnetism and liquid elements.

Line Integrals and Surface Integrals: Line integrals and surface integrals, ideas created through the expansion of math to various aspects, have applications in different regions like electromagnetism, liquid stream, and mathematical examination.

4. Differential Conditions

Standard Differential Conditions (Tributes): Tributes are utilized to display frameworks that develop regarding a solitary free factor. They have applications in regions like populace elements, mechanical frameworks, and electrical circuits. The techniques for settling Tributes created by Newton and Leibniz are as yet educated and applied today.

Halfway Differential Conditions (PDEs): PDEs expand the idea of differential conditions to elements of numerous factors and are fundamental to numerical material science, designing, and numerous different fields. The devices and procedures for settling PDEs depend vigorously on math ideas presented by Newton and Leibniz.

5. Applications in Material science and Designing

Old style Mechanics: Newton's math based standards of traditional mechanics, including his laws of movement and the law of general attraction, stay the underpinning of old style material science. These standards are utilized to depict the movement of items, planetary circles, and divine mechanics.

Electromagnetism: Math assumes a critical part in the investigation of electromagnetism, as planned by James Representative Maxwell in the nineteenth 100 years. The conditions of electromagnetism, known as Maxwell's situations, are communicated utilizing vector math and stay urgent in current physical science and designing.

Liquid Elements: Math based techniques are fundamental in liquid elements, a field that investigates the way of behaving of liquids (fluids and gases). Ideas like angles, twist, and uniqueness are utilized to demonstrate liquid stream, making math fundamental in understanding peculiarities like optimal design and hydrodynamics.

Quantum Mechanics: Quantum mechanics, the groundwork of present day material science, depends on numerical formalism that incorporates differential conditions and complex examination. These numerical devices are fundamental for depicting the way of behaving of particles at the quantum level.

Designing: Specialists use math to show and investigate many frameworks, from underlying designing and electrical circuits to compound responses and control frameworks. Analytics based methods are indispensable to the plan and streamlining of designing arrangements.

6. **Mathematical Strategies and Computational Science**

Mathematical Mix and Separation: Mathematical strategies for mix and separation are fundamental for taking care of issues in science and designing. These strategies give approximations to subordinates and integrals and are vital for programmatic experiences.

Limited Component Examination: Limited component examination (FEA) is a mathematical technique utilized in designing and physical science to tackle fractional differential conditions and reenact the way of behaving of mind boggling designs and materials. It depends on math ideas for addressing differential conditions mathematically.

7. **Likelihood and Measurements**

Likelihood Thickness Capabilities: Likelihood thickness capabilities (PDFs) and combined dispersion capabilities (CDFs), which are fundamental in likelihood hypothesis, frequently include math ideas. These capabilities portray the probability of irregular occasions happening inside a given reach.

Factual Examination: Math is utilized in measurable examination to determine most extreme probability assessors, perform theory tests, and foster models for information examination. Ideas like subsidiaries and integrals are applied to improve factual strategies.

8. High level Numerical Ideas

Utilitarian Investigation: Practical examination, a part of science that arrangements with vector spaces of capabilities, depends on math ideas to concentrate on straight administrators and spaces of capabilities. It has applications in quantum mechanics and the hypothesis of fractional differential conditions.

Differential Math: Differential calculation, which examines the properties of bends and surfaces in space, consolidates analytics based strategies to portray the math of manifolds. This field has applications in everyday relativity and mathematical demonstrating.

9. Instructing and Learning Science

Instructive Worth: The investigation of math improves understudies' insightful reasoning and critical thinking abilities. It gives significant preparation in numerical meticulousness and deliberation, abilities that are adaptable to different areas of math and science.

Passage to Higher Math: Math fills in as an entryway to cutting edge numerical trains like examination, variable based math, and geography. It gives the numerical establishment to chasing after additional particular areas of arithmetic.

10. Interdisciplinary Applications

AI and Man-made consciousness: Math is utilized in AI and computerized reasoning calculations, especially in improvement issues and angle based learning techniques. It supports the preparation of brain organizations and profound learning models.

Information Science: Math ideas are applied in information science for information examination, highlight designing, and model preparation. Procedures like slope drop and mathematical combination are utilized to tackle information related issues.

Biomedical Demonstrating: Math is instrumental in displaying natural and physiological cycles. It is utilized in pharmacokinetics, the study of disease transmission, and the investigation of perplexing organic frameworks.